Shooting Great Digital Photos

FOR

DUMMIES®

PORTABLE EDITION

by Mark Justice Hinton
with Barbara Obermeier

D0038829

WILEY

Wiley Publishing, Inc.

Shooting Great Digital Photos For Dummies® Portable Edition

Published by
Wiley Publishing, Inc.
111 River Street
Hoboken, NJ 07030-5774

www.wiley.com

Copyright © 2010 by Wiley Publishing, Inc., Indianapolis, Indiana

Published by Wiley Publishing, Inc., Indianapolis, Indiana

Published simultaneously in Canada

For general information on our other products and services, please contact our Customer Care Department within the U.S. at 877-762-2974, outside the U.S. at 317-572-3993, or fax 317-572-4002.

For technical support, please visit www.wiley.com/techsupport.

Wiley also publishes its books in a variety of electronic formats. Some content that appears in print may not be available in electronic books.

ISBN: 978-0-470-59144-4

Manufactured in the United States of America

10 9 8 7 6 5 4 3 2 1

WILEY

Table of Contents

Publisher's Acknowledgments

We're proud of this book; please send us your comments at
http://dummies.custhelp.com. For other comments,
please contact our Customer Care Department within the U.S.
at 877-762-2974, outside the U.S. at 317-572-3993, or fax
317-572-4002.

Some of the people who helped bring this book to market
include the following:

Acquisitions, Editorial

Project Editors: Nicole Sholly,
Jodi Jensen

Executive Editor: Steve Hayes

Copy Editor: Susan Christophersen

Editorial Manager: Kevin Kirschner

Composition Services

Senior Project Coordinator:
Kristie Rees

Layout and Graphics: Carl Byers

Proofreaders: Laura Albert,
Linda Seifert

Publishing and Editorial for Technology Dummies

    Richard Swadley, Vice President and Executive Group Publisher

    Andy Cummings, Vice President and Publisher

    Mary Bednarek, Executive Acquisitions Director

    Mary C. Corder, Editorial Director

Publishing for Consumer Dummies

    Diane Graves Steele, Vice President and Publisher

Composition Services

    Debbie Stailey, Director of Composition Services

Introduction

• •

Smile! Everybody say "cheese."

Photographs freeze a moment in time forever. Even an underexposed, out-of-focus photo may affect you as strongly as the finest photo art. Photographs fascinate and entertain. People like photos.

Whether you use a cell phone camera or a top-of-the-line professional model, the widespread availability of digital cameras has energized popular photography. At any moment — triumphant or embarrassing — you can be ready to capture the scene.

Some things about photography haven't changed with digital technology. Your pictures have a subject and a frame. You can compose your photo by following guidelines that go back farther than anyone reading this book can remember. However, digital photography has brought a few radical changes to photography:

- ✔ Photos are immediately accessible and shareable — no more delayed gratification
- ✔ Photos last forever — digital never fades or curls
- ✔ Technology makes things easy that used to be impossible by enabling you to stop action and capture great details

The phrase *point and shoot* promises an ease of use that most digital cameras deliver. But this simplicity also brings new challenges, such as what to do with the 20,000 digital photos stashed on your hard drive.

Your camera's Automatic mode almost guarantees that you'll take adequate photos under most circumstances. That mode leaves some room for improvement in your shots, however. Your camera has more sophisticated modes and settings, and this book tells you what they are and how to use them.

After the shot has been captured, you can still do more with the photo. A few simple edits can transform a photo from "okay" to "Wow!" You can share your snapshots or art with the world or with just a few friends.

About This Book

Taking good photographs does not require you to be exceptionally talented or studious. Neither should your photographs force your friends to yawn and make excuses to avoid looking at 300 similar shots from your vacation. The goal of this book is to help you enjoy taking pictures and to help you experiment with all the features of your camera, as well as to deal with your photos after the shot.

This book provides an overview that takes you from buying a camera to taking easy photos, to better photos, to sharing your photos. Along the way, we provide enough depth to help you gain confidence in your photographic endeavors. You won't find any long-winded lectures here ("Lens Caps: Impediment or Opportunity?"), but you will find helpful step-by-steps and friendly advice from folks with a lot of experience with digital cameras.

In this book, you discover how to

- ✔ Use your camera's preset scene modes to take your first photos
- ✔ Control exposure for just the right brightness
- ✔ Focus, as well as what the common guidelines are for composing your photos
- ✔ Photograph special subjects from portraits, to animals, to events, to landscapes

The book ends with ten handy tips for getting better photos.

Whom This Book Is For

You may already have your first digital camera, or you may be ready to get a new one and are looking for some guidance on what type of digital camera to buy. Perhaps you want to take advantage of your camera's automatic functions, but you're curious about what else your camera can do.

Icons Used in This Book

You may notice the little icons that appear in the left margin throughout the book. These are standard *For Dummies* road signs to give you some guidance along the way. They tell you, among other things, when to pay especially close attention, when to step lightly, and where to find additional information. Here's what they mean:

Look for this icon for something extra, some suggestion you can easily put into practice right away. These are the chocolate chips in the book's cookie.

Now and then, we want to remind you of something before we go on. We know you remember every word you read. We just want to be sure we didn't forget to mention something already.

When something pops up that could cause some trouble, such as "click Yes to delete all photos," we'll warn you about the consequences.

Chapter 1

Fast and Easy Picture Taking

● ●

In This Chapter

▶ Getting good-quality images

▶ Examining your camera's preset modes

▶ Finding the best light for your subject

▶ Having some fun with your camera

▶ Checking out the photos you've just taken

● ●

*W*ith camera in hand, you're ready to shoot. In this chapter, you learn enough to jump into using your camera with confidence. Before your first shot, set the image quality and get a sense of your camera's many automatic modes. Check out a few tips about light — photography is all about light and dark. And then take some fun shots before you review the photos on your camera's LCD.

Because of differences between camera makes and models, some setting names and locations may be different from what you find here. Be sure to have your camera's user manual handy, and remember that nothing beats getting out there and running your camera through its paces. Try every setting, take a shot, and see what happens: That's really the only way to truly feel comfortable with your camera.

Setting Image Quality

You want to take great photos, so make sure your camera is working with you. Set the image quality to yield the best photos and to give you maximum flexibility in editing and printing.

Image quality can be affected by two different settings: resolution and file format. For maximum flexibility after you've taken a photo, you want the highest resolution your camera is capable of, although that does produce the largest files. That means fewer photos will fit on your memory card. So you need to find a balance between resolution and file size. Use your camera's setup menu to see what options are available.

Figure 1-1 shows a sample Image Quality menu with quality options listed from highest to lowest (top to bottom) — and, in effect, file size from largest to smallest.

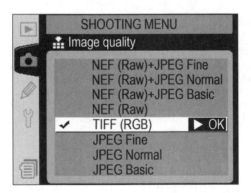

Figure 1-1: Choose a setting from the image quality menu.

You camera is likely to support the following three file formats:

- ✔ **JPEG/JPG:** This is the most widely used format for photographs. After all, JPEG originates with the Joint Photographic *Experts* Group. JPEG is designed to compress images in a very clever way by calculating what information you won't miss. JPEG compression varies by percentage, although most cameras don't specify a percentage. In Figure 1-1, notice the two options: JPEG Fine (which uses little or no compression) and JPEG Basic (which uses greater compression but probably still results in adequate quality except for the highest grade and largest prints). In between the two in size and quality is JPEG Normal.

  If file size isn't an issue, you want JPEG with the least compression. On the menu shown in Figure 1-1, for example, you would choose JPEG Fine.

- ✔ **TIFF/TIF:** This *tagged image file format* is an old format originally used for scanned images. There are variations on TIFF, including some with compression, but it is usually a *lossless* file type — no data is removed during compression — and files are large, which results in higher-quality images but fewer photos per memory card.

- ✔ **RAW:** This is the newest format and can vary among cameras. The goal of RAW is to capture more information — everything the image sensor sees. RAW might include additional copies of the image with different exposures or formats, such as RAW + JPEG.

So, is RAW best and JPEG worst? Not necessarily. Remember that you will be viewing these pictures on your computer, attaching them to e-mail, uploading them to the Web, and editing them for hours. Every program for working with or viewing photos handles JPEG easily. Only the latest software handles RAW. If you e-mail a huge RAW file to a friend, she may not be able to see it. JPEG gets points for longevity and ease of use, as well as smaller file size.

So, JPEG is best, right? Hold on. JPEG is lossy — JPEG compresses by throwing away data. If you repeatedly edit and save the same JPEG photo, you compress it more and more, eventually substantially degrading the quality.

For the record, Adobe, the maker of Photoshop and other photo editors, has created a RAW variant called Digital Negative (DNG). Microsoft has its own format, HD Photo. The question remains as to whether camera makers will adopt these formats.

 On some cameras, you can shoot both RAW and JPEG simultaneously, thereby giving you more options in postprocessing. Just be sure to have plenty of large-capacity memory cards on hand.

Not to belabor this point, but for flexibility in editing and printing, you want the image resolution plus the file format that together, not coincidentally, produce the largest files (because they contain more information). It's not that you want large files, but that you want the *benefits* of the information that makes those files larger. Complicating this issue is that large files take up more space (fewer photos per gigabyte), are slower to record to the memory card and to move around, and may not be as easy to work with as smaller files.

 While you're rooting around in the setup menu, look for a sound option that controls the sounds the camera makes. A shutter sound may provide

good feedback when you're shooting, but it may
also be disturbing, especially in a quiet setting.
You may be able to turn the sound down or off.

Using Preset Scene Modes

Your camera probably has various scene modes that
configure the camera for specific shooting conditions.
Using these modes is easy and may produce better
pictures — you just have to experiment.

Look for a mode dial, dedicated buttons, or menu
options. Figure 1-2 shows a mode dial set to A for
Automatic. Your camera may show Auto or a camera
icon. The Automatic mode setting is usually the only
green icon on the mode dial.

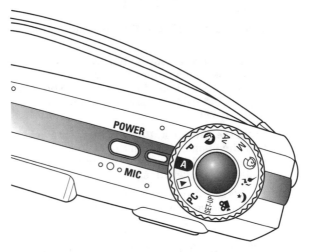

Figure 1-2: Pick from the preset scene modes.

Automatic mode does it all, of course. Don't be afraid to operate on Automatic. However, you will surely shoot in conditions in which other modes produce better pictures.

Landscape, Portrait, Night Sky, or Action/Sports modes may produce better pictures than Automatic under the corresponding circumstances.

 Take lots of pictures. Take the same picture several times, switching modes. See Chapter 2 to learn about Manual mode and other advanced settings.

The following steps guide you through taking your first photo. (You've already done this, haven't you?)

1. **Set the Mode dial or button to Automatic mode. In Automatic mode, your camera makes all the decisions.**

2. **Compose your shot in the viewfinder or LCD screen.**

3. **Press the shutter button halfway down to give your camera a moment to focus. This takes a fraction of a second, in most cases. You may see a green indicator on the LCD or electronic viewfinder (EVF).**

4. **Press the shutter button the rest of way to capture the image. (Writing the captured file to the memory card takes a fraction of a second — longer for bigger files.)**

5. **Switch to another scene mode and take the same picture. You can compare these versions later.**

 Play with different scene modes with the same subject. For more advice on using scene modes, see Chapter 3.

Shedding Some Light on Your Subject

Nothing is more important than light in photography. Or is darkness more important? In fact, a photo captures light and dark, as well as color. Photographers use numerous terms to describe the interplay of light and dark, such as exposure, contrast, and brightness.

Your camera's scene modes are preset for certain conditions of light and darkness. Start with the available light and consider the available modes. Eventually, you may want to add a separate light source (such as a flash) and delve deeper into your camera's controls.

Finding the light

Exposure refers to the amount of light that enters the lens. You can think about light in several ways, such as the direction, intensity (brightness), color, and *quality* of light. To incorporate these characteristics of light into your compositions, here are a few tips:

✔ **Time of day:** The best light for photographs is usually around dawn or dusk. The light is warmer and softer, and the shadows are longer and less harsh. Avoid midday light when the sun causes harsh or sharp shadows and squinting. If you must shoot at noon, move your subject into shady areas or turn your flash on to reduce shadows on faces. (This is called a *fill flash* or *forced flash*.)

Turn every rule or suggestion upside down to see for yourself whether it's valid. Have a shoot-out at high noon. Where some see ugly shadows, you may capture something strong or dramatic. (Remember, no one has to see your mistakes.)

When shooting indoors, try positioning your subject next to a window that doesn't have direct sunlight streaming through. You can also add light by using table lamps and overhead lights. Position the lights at a 45-degree angle to your subject, if possible.

✔ **Weather:** Cloudy or overcast days can be excellent for taking photos, especially portraits. The light is soft and diffused. An empty sky may be less interesting than one with clouds. Keep in mind that overcast days are especially useful for photographing people, as shown in Figure 1-3.

Photo credit: Purestock

Figure 1-3: Shoot in soft, outdoor light.

✔ **Direction:** Photographing a subject with *back-lighting* (lighting that comes from behind) can produce a dramatic image, as shown in Figure 1-4. Avoid *lens flare* — those nasty light circles or rainbow effects that mar images — by not having your brightest light source shine directly into your lens.

Be careful shooting photos when the light source is directly behind your subject. Your camera may adjust the light meter to the lighter background and not to your subject, thereby creating an overly dark foreground or subject. If the exposure of the foreground subject is good, a bright background may be too bright in the photo. The effect is dramatic when intentional but awful when unintentional. Consider forcing the flash, if necessary.

Photo credit: Digital Vision

Figure 1-4: Use backlighting creatively in an image.

✔ **Color:** The light at midday is white, the light at sunrise and sunset is orange and feels warm, and the light in shaded areas and at twilight is blue and appears cool.

Your camera's modes may *push* color in different directions in an effort to enhance the image.

✔ **Creative:** When possible, use lighting creatively to lead the eye, create a mood, or evoke an emotion. Look for compositions created with light illuminating or shadowing an object.

Using contrast

Contrast describes the degree of difference between light and dark areas. High contrast defines stark differences between light and dark areas; low contrast appears softer and more muted.

Mixing light with dark provides contrast, which in turns creates impact, as shown in Figure 1-5.

To highlight contrast in a photo composition, just be sure that the high-contrast area of your image is also the focal point, because that's where the eye looks first.

In color images, you can also achieve contrast by using complementary colors, such as red and green, yellow and blue, and cyan and orange. Look for contrast in both nature and your own setups.

Even basic photo editors enable changes to brightness and contrast after the fact. A too-dark or too-bright photo may be repairable.

Photo credit: PhotoDisc

Figure 1-5: Contrasting light and
dark creates impact.

Taking Some Fun Shots

Without delving any deeper into your camera's controls or photography's bigger picture (sorry, couldn't
resist the pun), you can easily move beyond the standard snapshot (Although snapshots have their place,
and not every picture needs to be art.)

You should look into (they're coming frequently
now) changing your perspective. Get closer to a tiny

subject with your macro setting. Bring a distant subject closer to you with zoom. Squat, crouch, stretch to
put the lens higher or lower than standing height.

For every photograph you take, you always have an
initial decision: whether to hold your camera horizon-
tally (*landscape*, which is how it hangs from the
straps) or to turn it vertically (*portrait*). That's a key
decision, and you base it in large part on the shape of
the scene: Do you want to include more vertical or
horizontal area in the picture? Which perspective suits
the subject? You might think portrait suits a person,
but what if the scene around them is important?
Consider landscape in that case. (Take both.) You'd
have to think landscape for a landscape — duh — but
what if you want to lead the eye up a valley or along a
ridge you're standing on? Try portrait to emphasize
the depth or length. (Take both.)

One of the simplest edits is to crop a picture,
which means that you save the part you want
and throw the rest away. Cropped photos can
be square or use other proportions than those
of a standard print.

Shooting close-ups in Macro mode

How close can you put your lens to an object and still
take a clear photo? Many cameras have a separate
Macro mode to enable you to photograph objects
within inches — even less than an inch, for some.
Look for a flower symbol on the camera body.

A macro exposure makes the small large — even
huge. Figure 1-6 shows a close-up of a one-inch June
bug on a chamisa bush. The original scene is barely
two inches square, but it fills a computer monitor
larger than life.

Photo credit: Mark Justice Hinton

Figure 1-6: Set your camera to Macro mode for close-up shots.

You may need to experiment with exposure settings. Start with Automatic or the Sports setting (for things that move fast, such as bugs or flowers in a breeze).

Don't use a flash with macros. A flash won't do any good that close and may ruin the shot. If your flash is set to Auto, you may have to suppress it (turn it off).

For flowers and small creatures, you may want to get on your knees or stomach for a good shot. A movable LCD can spare you that effort by flipping up or out.

The closer you get to the subject, the greater the odds that you'll actually bump into it or cast a shadow over the subject. Even a breath of air can move the subject and cause blurring. Consider placing the camera on the ground or a mini-tripod and using the self-timer.

Check your camera's documentation to find out the particular focusing distance that Macro mode is capable of.

Follow these steps to take a macro exposure:

1. **Set the Mode dial or button to Macro on your camera. Look for a flower icon.**

2. **Compose your shot in the viewfinder or LCD screen. Focusing in Macro mode can be tricky, so be sure that the subject you want is in focus; if it's not, make the necessary adjustments.**

3. **Press the shutter button halfway to give your camera a moment to establish the shot.**

4. **Press the shutter button the rest of way to capture the image.**

Shooting from unexpected angles

To see the world differently, change the way you look at it. Get down (or up). Walk around your subject, if you can, crouching and stretching. Try not to frighten people in the process.

Take some photos from angles other than straight on at five to six feet off the ground — the world of the average snapshot. Changing your viewpoint can exaggerate the size of the subject either larger or smaller, enhance the mood of the shot, or make a dull shot more interesting, as shown in Figure 1-7.

Photo credit: Mark Justice Hinton

Figure 1-7: Use an unexpected angle to exaggerate a subject. (Don't push the button!)

Depending on your particular subject, try a bird's-eye view (above the subject) or a worm's-eye view (below it).

 Most flower photos are face on and nice enough. Try photographing flowers from the side or the back in the morning or evening (avoiding lens flare) — people seldom see this perspective.

Zooming in on your subject

Whereas a macro shot gets you closer to something that's already close by, a telephoto shot brings the distant object close to you. Strictly speaking, a *tele-photo* lens has a fixed focal length. A *zoom* lens is a magical lens that easily ranges from normal to tele-photo and every step in between. On your camera, look for a long switch labeled *W* (for wide angle — normal) at one end and *T* (telephoto) at the other (this kind of switch is called a *rocker*).

Gently press the *T* end of this odd switch while look-ing through the viewfinder or LCD. Zoom. With your eye glued to the camera, press the *W* end. Zoom back. An electronic viewfinder or LCD may display the degree of zoom or magnification from 1x (normal) to the maximum for your camera (10x is 10 times closer than normal; 20x is the current maximum).

Follow these steps to zoom:

1. **Focus on your subject and press the Zoom button until you achieve the framing you want.**

2. **Compose your shot and press the shutter button.**

3. **If your camera has an image-stabilization fea-ture (often a waving hand), be sure that it's acti-vated to help eliminate camera shake and the resulting image blur. (Automatic mode proba-bly turns image stabilization on.) A tripod is helpful with a long zoom, especially in less bright conditions.**

   Some DSLR manufacturers recommend turning off image-stabilization (IS) if you are using a tripod. IS compensates for small movements; it may misbehave when there are no small move-ments to compensate for (as is the case when you use a tripod). Check your camera documen-tation. (Don't bother tapping the tripod to intro-duce vibrations to keep the IS happy.)

Keep in mind that zooming in with an optical zoom shortens the depth of field (DOF). An *optical* lens uses the optics of the camera (the lens) to bring the subject closer. (Chapter 2 discusses DOF in depth. Ahem.) Objects outside the DOF — nearer or farther — will be out of focus; the background may become blurrier, as shown in the close-up of a coreopsis flower in front of a green lawn in Figure 1-8. Make sure that this effect is what you want. This out-of-focus effect is called *bokeh*, from a Japanese word meaning *blurry* or *fuzzy*.

Photo credit: Mark Justice Hinton

Figure 1-8: Zoom in to your image.

 Lenses with optical zooms are real zoom lenses. The lens actually brings the subject closer. A digital zoom isn't actually a zoom lens. It simply enlarges the center of the scene in the camera and crops out the rest. And a digital zoom can degrade image resolution and quality. If quality is paramount, you want to avoid using a digital zoom. You may have to disable the digital zoom by using a menu option or avoid pressing the zoom past the optical maximum setting.

There are three ways to fill a frame with your subject. One is to zoom in from a distance until it fills the frame. Another is to get as close as possible, using Macro mode, if necessary. The third is to crop the subject out of a larger frame. You should try taking the same picture all three ways to get a better feel for the impact of your choice on exposure, background, and focus.

Holding Hollywood in your hands

Most digital cameras take movies, too. Look for a symbol that looks like a piece of film with sprocket holes down both sides, an old school reel-to-reel camera icon, or a box camera on a tripod.

With the dial set to Movie mode, press and release the shutter button to start recording a movie. You'll see a Record indicator on the EVF or LCD — look for a red circle or REC. The movie will continue to record until you press the shutter button a second time (or, until the disk fills or a fixed file size limit is reached). Some cameras allow you to pause and resume the same movie; most cameras create separate movies each time you start and stop.

Some cameras record sound with movies. Some cameras allow you to zoom in and out while making a movie. You just need to experiment to see what you can do with yours.

Your camera's setup menu may have a setting for frames per second (fps) — 30 fps or more is smoothest. You may also be able to choose a movie size or resolution — 640 by 480 pixels or greater is good.

An unsteady movie may nauseate your audience. Most movies taken with a digital still camera should be pretty short (up to 5 minutes) without too much walking around. A tripod will make movies steadier.

Typically, movie files are stored as AVI or MOV (QuickTime) files. These files are huge.

For an example of a movie, see Figure . . . wait, that's not going to work. Check out www.mjhinton.com/DCPFD for a short movie of hummingbirds around a feeder in Colorado.

 If you're really serious about great movie making, you probably want a digital video camera and good movie editing software. For more information, see *Digital Video For Dummies,* 4th Edition, by Keith Underdahl (published by Wiley).

Reviewing Photos on Your Camera

You may want to see — and show — the pictures you've taken while they're still in your camera. That's instant gratification. Last century, people mailed film to a lab and waited weeks for their photos to come back on shiny bits of paper! A common reaction then was, "Why did I take that?"

If your camera has both an electronic viewfinder and an LCD, you can see your photos on either. The LCD will be better, of course, but remember that your batteries are draining.

Some cameras automatically show the most recent picture you took for a few seconds. You may be able to turn that feature on or off in the setup menus.

(It can be distracting if you quickly shoot several pictures in a row.)

To review photos, look for the one button you haven't used so far, which may have a triangle on it. In Review mode, other buttons change function to enable you to move forward and back or, possibly, to see more than one photo at one time. Zoom may even zoom into the picture.

 Don't bother to delete or edit photos on the camera. Move them to your computer, instead.

Some cameras can connect to TVs using standard RCA or USB cables, allowing you to run a slide show on the TV. (That's a great time to have a wireless remote.) You probably don't want to show every picture on your memory card, though.

Chapter 2

Getting the Right Exposure

• •

In This Chapter

▶ Controlling the shutter speed

▶ Getting comfortable with aperture settings

▶ Being sensitive to ISO

▶ Working with a tripod

• •

*L*ook off at a spot exactly four feet in front of your face. (Okay, look around first to make sure no one is watching.) How hard is that? Now, using your eyes — not your camera — make everything five feet away blurry. Can't do it? Cameras can do that: focus precisely and vary the depth of field (DOF) — really the depth of *focus*, with blurring nearer and farther than the DOF.

The point is, the lens isn't really just an extension of your eye. Cameras and eyes (plus brains) have very different optics and follow different rules. You don't have to master camera optics, but you need to be aware that certain factors can affect what you get out of your camera.

This chapter can help you move out of the preset scene modes into various manual options. You start to juggle settings that the scene modes handle automatically for you.

For now, your most important task is to get to know your camera. Become familiar with how your camera works as you become more comfortable with the fundamentals of photography. Remember that you have no film to process, so get out there and push those buttons.

Understanding Exposure

Exposure refers to the amount of light allowed to fall on the image sensor in the camera during image capture. Exposure is the result of the combination of the length of time that the image sensor receives light (*shutter speed*), the size of the lens opening (*aperture*), and the light sensitivity of your image sensor. The next few sections tell you more about each of these settings.

Figure 2-1 shows the physical relationship of four hardware components. Light passes through the lens. The amount of light that enters the camera beyond the lens is controlled by the aperture. How long that aperture admits light is controlled by the shutter. Whatever light the aperture and shutter let in strikes the image sensor, whose sensitivity to that amount of light is modifiable. The image sensor translates light into digital information that is then written to your memory card.

Figure 2-2 represents the range between darker and lighter exposure. Each setting listed individually in the figure pushes exposure lighter or darker.

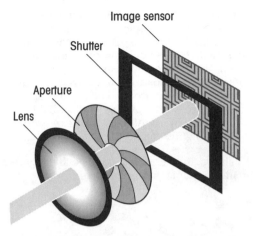

Figure 2-1: Light passes through the lens, aperture, and shutter to strike the image sensor.

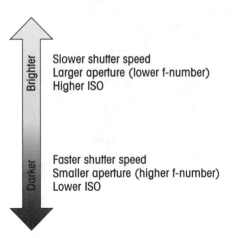

Figure 2-2: Changing one setting changes exposure.

If you change just one of the three settings I just mentioned — say, shutter speed — you change the exposure. Increased shutter speed decreases exposure. That's ideal if the scene is very bright, but it's not so good if the light is dim because there isn't enough time for the exposure. *Underexposure* translates into a darker image. Decreased shutter speed increases exposure, which is good for low light but washes out a photo in bright light. *Overexposure* translates into a lighter image.

Figure 2-3 shows an overexposed image and Figure 2-4 shows an image that is underexposed.

Figure 2-3: An overexposed image.

Figure 2-4: An underexposed image.

 People react to photographs. Light affects mood and emotion. A bright scene may be uplifting; a dark scene may evoke somberness or look strikingly dramatic.

As you see in each of the following sections, your camera lets you control one variable while it adjusts the others. In terms of Figure 2-2, as you push a setting in one direction, the camera will push another setting in the other direction to try for balanced exposure. Manual mode enables you to change more than one setting and to choose a combination the camera might not choose. (Results can be good or bad, in that case.)

Setting the shutter speed

The shutter has to open for any exposure to take place. That's why your camera has a shutter button — to trigger the opening of the shutter. How long the shutter remains open after you click that button is determined by the shutter speed setting. Outside on a sunny day, a faster shutter speed may be necessary to avoid overexposure. As the sun sets, you may want to use a slower shutter speed for the same level of exposure.

Shutter speeds are measured in fractions of seconds or whole seconds and usually range from 30 seconds to $\frac{1}{4000}$, or sometimes even $\frac{1}{8000}$, of a second. Some cameras also have a B (Bulb) mode, which enables you to keep the shutter open as long as you hold down the button.

Another consideration in setting shutter speed is whether anything in the scene is moving. When you're using slower shutter speeds and a stationary camera, objects in motion will blur. Higher shutter speeds freeze the action.

 A camera's Sports mode automatically sets a higher shutter speed for action shots. Take advantage of that when photographing wildlife.

If your camera has Shutter Priority mode (most likely S or SP on the mode dial), use it to specify the shutter speed to use. In this mode, your camera automatically adjusts the aperture, which I discuss in the next section. When you choose a slower shutter speed, the exposure gets more time. Consequently, your camera automatically chooses a smaller aperture to admit less light for the exposure, avoiding overexposure. Conversely, choosing a faster shutter speed allows less time for the exposure, and your camera chooses a larger aperture to admit more light in the time available to avoid underexposure.

Keep the following in mind when you're setting shutter speed:

- ✔ Set the shutter speed by turning the dial located on the front or top of your camera and looking at the LCD display. On the Mode menu or dial, choose Shutter Priority mode, which may be labeled as S, SP, or Tv (as in *time value*). Setting your camera to Shutter Priority mode enables you to manually set the shutter speed while the camera determines all other settings. If you can't locate the dial, check your camera's user manual to see if your camera offers this mode.

- ✔ Look for an indicator in your EVF or on the LCD that confirms that the camera settings are within an approved programmed range. You may see a green light if the settings are acceptable or a red light if the settings are not acceptable.

- ✔ The brighter the scene, the faster the shutter speed you can use, such as $\frac{1}{4000}$. For speeds slower than $\frac{1}{60}$ of a second, you should use a tripod to avoid camera shake and to ensure a sharp image. If you don't have a tripod and your camera has an image-stabilization feature, be sure to turn it on for slower shutter speeds.

- ✔ Keep in mind that when you use Shutter Priority mode, the aperture adjusts automatically. So, you don't have to worry about setting it manually.

- ✔ To intentionally blur an image with a moving subject (*motion blur*), set the shutter speed to a slower speed. To freeze the action in a shot, use a faster speed.

- ✔ When using a longer lens, you may need to increase the shutter speed to keep photos sharp. As a guideline, use a speed that's larger than the lens focal length. For example, if you're using a 55mm lens, anything over $\frac{1}{60}$ is acceptable.

Figure 2-5 shows the blurring or motion effect possible with a slower shutter speed.

Photo credit: PhotoDisc

Figure 2-5: Set the shutter speed to a slower setting to blur an image.

Figure 2-6 shows action stopped by a higher shutter speed.

Changing the aperture

Like the iris in your eye, a camera lens can open wide or be narrowed to the size of a pin prick. The lens opening is the aperture. A wide aperture lets in more light. A narrow aperture lets in less light. As you walk through a dark room, your iris's aperture widens to let you see the dog that you're about to trip over. Flip

on the light and your iris's aperture narrows quickly
to reduce the flood of light.

Photo credit: PhotoDisc

Figure 2-6: Set the shutter speed to
a faster setting to freeze movement.

A bright scene might call for a narrower aperture,
whereas a dimmer scene may need a wider aperture.
When you use a scene mode such as Cloudy or Night
Sky, your camera chooses a wider aperture to let in
more light because those are likely to be dimmer
scenes. When you choose a beach or landscape scene
mode, the camera automatically chooses a narrower
aperture to reduce the light because those are likely
to be bright scenes.

Another consideration is that aperture affects depth
of field (DOF), the range in which objects are in focus.

(Objects outside the DOF — both closer and farther than the subject of the photo — are out of focus.) The narrower the aperture, the deeper the DOF. The wider the aperture, the shallower the DOF.

Words like narrower or shallower seem vague until you fully appreciate the dimension or direction being discussed. Aperture is like a window. A narrow window lets in less light than a wide window. DOF is like a clear patch on a foggy road. The more of the road ahead you can see beyond your headlights, the deeper the DOF.

Not surprisingly, DOF conveys depth. Photography converts three dimensions into two. A deep DOF can emphasize distance. Figure 2-7 ranges from a nearby ruin (in Hovenweep National Monument, Utah), across a valley toward a distant mountain range. This is the deep DOF that comes from a small aperture.

Photo credit: Mark Justice Hinton

Figure 2-7: Small aperture; deep DOF — miles deep.

You may want a shallow DOF to emphasize your subject by blurring objects in the background or foreground that distract. Figure 2-8 shows the shallow DOF that comes from a large aperture. The white apache plume flowers are in focus, but objects nearer and farther away are not.

Photo credit: Mark Justice Hinton

Figure 2-8: Large aperture, shallow DOF.

This is the tricky aspect of DOF. Focus is not just on a single point or plane in space. There is a range nearer and farther than the subject that is also in focus. If your DOF is 6 feet and your subject is 3 feet away, everything between you and the subject and 3 feet beyond is in focus. With the same depth of field and a subject that is 30 feet away, the effect is quite different. Consider Figure 2-7 again. Imagine if the valley were in focus but the ruins were not — that would be the case with a shallow DOF. Keep that same shallow DOF and focus on the ruins and nothing in the valley will be distinct.

On a cloudy day or in a room lit only by daylight coming through windows, you might need to widen the aperture to get enough exposure. However, that wider aperture reduces the DOF, increasing the odds that some part of the scene falls outside the focus and is blurry or fuzzy. That's not necessarily bad — you can use that effect intentionally.

Aperture is measured in *f stops*. For example, f2.8 is a wide-open lens, admitting lots of light (with less DOF), whereas f8.0 is a narrow opening, admitting less light than f2.8 (but with greater DOF than f2.8). Every f stop has a specific DOF associated with it.

Notice the paradox of f stops: the higher the number, the narrower the aperture. That's because an f stop is a ratio (hang in there) of the width of the lens opening to the focal length of the lens. Traditionally, f2.8 is written as *f/2.8*; the lowercase *f* is the focal length and the aperture is the result of dividing the focal length of the lens by 2.8. As the f stop number (the divisor, really) gets higher, the aperture gets narrower. An aperture of f4 (or f/4) divides the focal length by four. One fourth is smaller than 1/2.8; f4 is narrower than f2.8; f8 is narrower still (1/8). With each step from f2.8 to f4 to f5.6 to f8, the aperture is narrower, admitting less light (and the DOF grows deeper with each step).

Interestingly, each f stop admits twice as much light as the next *higher* f stop and half as much light as the next *lower* f stop. (Relax, there won't be a quiz.)

If your camera has an Aperture Priority mode (usually an A or AP on the mode dial), use it to set the aperture you want and your camera automatically adjusts the shutter speed.

Shutter speed affects the freezing or blurring of moving objects within a scene.

All these details make you appreciate Automatic mode, don't they? But keep in mind that Automatic mode can't push the settings to change the mood or emphasize one part of the scene.

 Your LCD or EVF will show you whether the scene is brighter or darker as you adjust aperture. You won't see the effect on DOF, however. DSLRs may have a preview button that shows DOF.

Keep these things in mind as you work with the aperture settings on your camera:

✔ Set the aperture by turning the dial (located on the front or top) and looking at the LCD display. On the Mode menu or dial, choose Aperture Priority mode, which may be labeled as A or Av (with the latter standing for *aperture value*). Setting your camera to Aperture Priority mode enables you to manually set the aperture while the camera determines all other settings. If you can't locate the dial, check your camera's user manual to see if your camera offers this mode.

✔ Look for an indicator in your EVF or on the LCD that the camera settings are within an approved programmed range. The indicator might be a green light (which means the settings are within range) or a red light (which means the settings are out of the approved range).

✔ The brighter the scene, the narrower the aperture you can use, meaning a higher-numbered f stop — as high as f8.0. For wider apertures (lower-numbered f stops), you should use a tripod to avoid camera shake and to ensure a sharp image. If you don't have a tripod and your camera has an image-stabilization feature,

> be sure to turn it on for wider apertures/lower
> f stops.
>
> ✔ Keep in mind that when you use Aperture
>   Priority the shutter speed adjusts automatically.

Setting ISO

Before digital cameras, film was described as
fast — very sensitive to light and fast to expose — or
slow — less sensitive to light and slow to expose.

The standards for grading film's light sensitivity or
film speed were established by the International
Organization of Standards (ISO, an abbreviation taken
from the French name of the organization). Although
ISO is not a unit of measure, light sensitivity is graded
in terms of ISO. Here, a bigger number indicates
greater light sensitivity and faster exposure (and
overexposure); a smaller number indicates less light
sensitivity and slower exposure (or underexposure).

Although your digital camera doesn't use film, your
camera's image sensor clearly is sensitive to light.
And that sensitivity can be expressed as ISO.

Your camera has either a fixed ISO or chooses the ISO
automatically based on conditions. You may be able
to manually adjust the ISO. As you raise the ISO, you
increase sensitivity — good for lower light. As you
lower the ISO, you decrease sensitivity — good for
normal or brighter light. Cameras often operate automatically around ISO 100 in most levels of daylight.
ISO 1000 is very sensitive to light and might be appropriate for night shots with a tripod.

Vestiges of prior technology often carry forward into
newer technology. What does clockwise mean any-
more? Why do we still say that we dial our pushbut-
ton phones? Likewise, ISO has been brought forward

into the current age. Which is not to say that ISO is archaic. ISO provides a transition from old to new.

The dark side of using high ISO film is the resulting texture of a photo. Exposures at higher ISO tend to be grainy, speckled, or uneven because the increased sensitivity of high ISO film comes from larger grains of silver halide. The smaller, finer grains of lower ISO film produce smoother images.

Although digital cameras aren't subject to the chemistry of film, high ISO still has problems. The increased sensitivity of a high ISO digital setting increases interference and degrades the sharpness of photos. This interference is called *noise.* Noise is especially noticeable as defects in enlargements. Higher ISO may be noisier than low ISO settings, much as higher ISO film is grainier than low ISO film. To reduce degradation of the image, the highest ISO settings will surely require a tripod.

The practical significance of ISO is not merely that you may be able to shoot in low light. Higher ISO increases light sensitivity and that makes available narrower apertures (greater DOF) or faster shutter speeds than would be possible with lower ISO at low light. Settings that would underexpose a given ISO setting will adequately expose a higher ISO. An added benefit is that you may be able to shoot in low light without a tripod.

Understandably, you want your photos to have good exposure — not too bright, not too dark. ISO, aperture, and shutter speed are interrelated in regard to exposure. You can achieve the same level of exposure with different combinations of these settings. One of those combinations might result in more or less DOF. Another might freeze or blur motion. The exposure might be the same in each of these instances, but your options are different.

In the various preset modes, such as Automatic or Night Sky, your camera selects an ISO setting according to the lighting in the shot, as well as the aperture and shutter speed.

Go ahead, play with your ISO. Here are some things to think about as you play around with this setting:

- ✔ Look around until you find the ISO option on your camera. Because it's a less frequently adjusted setting, ISO may not be located with the other, more common options. (Many compact cameras don't let you change the ISO setting.)

- ✔ Press the ISO button and take a look at the ISO menu on your camera's LCD. Try setting the ISO speed. ISO speeds usually run at 50, 100, 200, 400, 800, 1600, or 3200.

- ✔ The lower the number of the ISO, the less sensitive your image sensor is to light. A low ISO number results in a photo with very fine grain. An ISO setting of 100 is considered average, but a low ISO speed may not work in low-light scenarios. Normally, you want the lowest ISO setting possible for best quality, unless you want a grainy shot for creative reasons.

- ✔ A high ISO number makes your image sensor more sensitive to light and creates a grainy, "noisy" image. High ISO settings may be necessary in low-light situations, especially when you're using a faster shutter speed, a narrower aperture, or both — for example, when you're shooting a moving subject inside a building.

- ✔ As with the other settings, you should take several similar shots, varying just the ISO setting. You may not be able to see any difference on your LCD. You're more likely to see differences on a computer screen.

Shooting in Manual mode

You can find ultimate control of your camera when you use Manual mode. This mode enables you to set each of the options discussed so far (shutter speed, aperture, and ISO). If you can juggle, you can use Manual mode.

When you use the semi-manual options, such as Shutter Priority, you select your desired shutter speed and the camera sets everything else based on that speed to produce a shot that is neither under- nor overexposed.

With Manual mode, you can override the adjustments the camera would make based on your semi-manual choices. For example, with Shutter Priority, as you increase shutter speed, you reduce the time for light to expose the image. Therefore, the camera increases aperture to let more light in — reducing the DOF or increasing the noise, in the process. (The camera could change ISO, instead of aperture, to suit conditions and your shutter speed.)

In Manual mode, however, you can increase shutter speed and reduce aperture at the same time, something the camera would not do as you adjust only one setting. Faster shutter speed with narrower aperture will underexpose most images and may create a dramatic effect. That would also produce greater DOF than if you set a fast shutter speed and the camera automatically opened the aperture. If you manually increase the ISO at the same time, you change options even further.

Continue to play with the various manual settings. Trial and error will teach you something about the synergy of these settings.

With the semi-manual modes, such as Aperture
Priority, you select the mode on the dial. To change
the aperture, you use a different control, perhaps a
wheel, lever, or dial. You'd use the same control with
Shutter Priority mode. However, in Manual Mode, you
can change multiple settings, so your camera provides a way to identify which setting you're changing
at a given moment. Look for prompts on the LCD or
EVF. The setting you are adjusting will be highlighted
in some way. When in doubt, read the manual.

Figure 2-9 displays Manual mode — indicated by M
in the upper-left corner — and other settings. The
shutter speed is 125 and the aperture is f13.

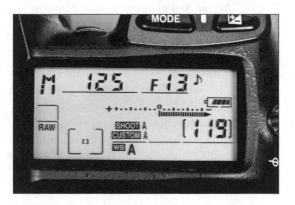

Figure 2-9: Set your camera to Manual mode to take
control of your settings.

Some of the buttons on your camera change
function depending on mode or other settings. A
common configuration on many cameras places
four semicircular buttons around a button. Each
of the smaller buttons has a dedicated function,
such as Macro or Flash. In Manual mode, those

buttons might move the selection highlight from one setting to the next. In Review mode, the same buttons might move you left and right through your photos.

The following steps walk you through turning on Manual mode and taking a photo using those settings:

1. **Set the Mode dial or button to M (Manual mode) on your camera.**

2. **In Manual mode, make all decisions about setting aperture, shutter speed, and ISO. As you watch the LCD or EVF, select aperture and change it. You should see the scene turn darker or lighter. Select shutter speed and change it, watching the exposure change.**

   This preview is not 100% accurate in predicting what you'll actually get, but you will at least see some effect of changes to settings.

   The first few times you use Manual mode, be sure to try it in a casual situation that isn't a once-in-a-lifetime event such as a birth or a wedding. Consider taking some duplicate shots in Automatic mode.

3. **Compose your shot in the viewfinder or LCD screen.**

4. **Press the shutter button halfway to give your camera a moment to establish the shot.**

5. **Press the shutter button the rest of the way to capture the image.**

 If your camera has a Program mode (P), you can set shutter speed and aperture at the same time rather than controlling one while the camera controls the other. Program mode stands between Automatic mode (the camera decides everything) and Manual mode (you decide everything).

Using a Tripod

Back in the days when Abraham Lincoln posed for the great photojournalist Mathew B. Brady, the subject of a photograph had to hold still while the photographer worked magic under a black cloth, muttering incantations and mixing potions. ("Eye of silver, tail of halide. . .")

A century and a half later, cameras are nearly small enough to strap to the back of a fly. Many of our subjects are in motion, and so are we (the photographers). Some conditions, however, still require holding the camera more still than most people are capable of holding it without assistance.

Many of the settings discussed in the preceding section of this chapter increase the odds of blurring, especially in low light. Furthermore, under less-than-ideal conditions, the slightest motion of the camera can introduce blur. (Try holding your camera rock-steady as you lean over a wall to photograph the running of the bulls. Picture abstract blurs with horns.)

The slightest camera movement is even more significant when you use a zoom lens that's fully extended or you use any lens in low light.

To diminish the possibility of undesirable blurring, many cameras provide some means of image stabilization. The lens may be isolated from movement by gyroscopes or special materials. The image sensor may be programmed — it's a computer chip, after all — to detect vibration and subtract that vibration from the final image.

Cameras with an image stabilization feature use it automatically. You may be able to turn it off, but you probably don't want to do that, except to experiment.

Despite the wonders of image stabilization, you may want to buy a tripod, the venerable tool of photography that even Mathew B. Brady would recognize after all these years.

Brady might be surprised by the variations in tripods, however. There are large tripods ranging from two to six feet tall with legs that fold or telescope. You may be able to set such a tripod at different heights using a twist or catch locking mechanism. Some tripods have pivoting connections so that you can incline the camera up, down, or sideways. You may even be able to remove the tripod head to hang it under the tripod (like a pot of beans over a campfire) for macro shots.

When is a tripod not a tripod? When it's a *monopod*. As you would expect, a monopod has a single leg — it's a walking stick with a camera connection. (Look for a monopod at a sporting goods or outdoor store if you often take your camera hiking.) Don't try to balance a monopod like a unicycle. Brace the monopod with your body or another stable object. The monopod's advantage over a tripod is that it is easier and faster to use and to move. Monopods are recommended over tripods when running with bulls.

Everyone needs a small tripod, something pocket-sized, for sheer convenience. And another small tripod style you might want to consider consists of a beanbag with a tripod connection for a malleable but stable bundle. (A beanbag drapes over a rock nicely.) Have I convinced you yet that you need a tripod?

Tripods are also useful for self-portraits and for group shots that you want to join. Use the self-timer and try not to trip over the tripod as you run to get in the shot. I don't mean that only as a joke — some cameras actually come with both short and long self-timer settings for your safety. So be sure to choose the setting that gives you enough time to get safely into the shot. Tripods are especially handy for taking movies, where any movement can be very distracting.

 If you need a tripod but don't have one handy, you can try placing the camera on something steady, such as a wall. Or, brace yourself against a solid object such as a tree or a large rock. Opinions differ about holding your breath as you click. (Seriously.) You could also increase the ISO to allow for a faster shutter speed or smaller aperture.

When you have a real tripod available and are ready to put it to use, follow these steps to use it successfully:

1. **Attach your camera to the tripod by screwing the tripod screw into the mount under the camera body.**

   Some tripods come equipped with a quick-connect plate that detaches from the tripod. If your tripod is so equipped, attach the plate to your camera ahead of time and use it to quickly attach and detach from the tripod.

2. **Establish the height of your tripod by adjusting the legs and neck of the tripod. Be sure to lock the legs and neck so that they don't slip. Get the height right to avoid straining your own neck as you compose the shot.**

3. **Adjust the head of the tripod until you have the exact angle you want for the camera.**

4. **Use the LCD screen and check the height and angle. Make any necessary adjustments.**

5. **If you're using a lens with an Image Stabilization or Vibration Reduction setting, you may want to turn that setting off when**

using a tripod (unless the lens also has a setting for detecting tripods).

Image Stabilization and Vibration Reduction settings enable you to hold a camera and decrease the incidence of camera shake. When you use a tripod, however, these settings can cause your photos to be blurry if the image stabilization feature actually tries to compensate for movement or shake that doesn't exist. (Ironic, isn't it?) Check your owner's manual for suggestions on using tripods with image stabilization.

Tripods are especially vital for taking shots that require the shutter speed to be slower, thereby helping to eliminate camera shake. Slower shutter speeds, which enable you to use wider aperture settings, are often used in low-light situations, such as bad weather, sunsets, and nighttime. You will also want to use one when using a telephoto or an ultrazoom lens.

Chapter 3

Composing Better Shots

●●●●●●●●●●●●●●●●●●●●●●●●●●●●●●●●●●●

In This Chapter

▶ Bringing your images into focus

▶ Understanding depth of field

▶ Determining your focal point

▶ Boning up on the Rule of Thirds

▶ Finding balance in your photos

●●●●●●●●●●●●●●●●●●●●●●●●●●●●●●●●●●●

*O*ne of the great things about digital photography is that it doesn't require a lot of thought. You can simply point your camera and click the shutter. (Okay, you do have to remember to turn it one and remove the lens cap, if the camera doesn't do that *automagically*.)

A camera is like a computer. Wait, that's a good thing! A camera has capabilities that you can ignore as long as you like. When you start looking deeper, you find more and more that you can do with your camera.

Even if you're using the simplest point-and-shoot camera without any extra options, you still control the shot. You select the subject and frame it within your view finder.

In this chapter, you look through the lens to see something new. You also explore various ideas for composing a photo to maximize your subject and minimize distractions.

Seeing through the Lens

Focus is vital in photography. A picture in focus is sharp and clear. A picture with the subject out-of-focus is probably a dud.

One problem with focusing a camera is that you're focusing your eye on something right in front of your face (the EVF or LCD), whereas your camera is focusing on the subject (you hope). Putting a lens (and everything else) between your eye and the subject requires seeing things in a slightly different way. It may help to understand how cameras focus and what you can do to control that.

Nailing your focus

When you raise your eyes from this page to look across the room, you continuously focus on whatever you're looking at. You don't think about fixing focus, unless you just woke up.

Most cameras don't work the way your eyes do, unless you change an option in setup. You can think of camera focus as consisting of three parts: when to focus, where in the frame to focus, and the distance between you and the subject. Each of these three elements can be handled by the camera or by you through your camera's setup menu or other controls.

When to focus

Normally, your camera only focuses when you press the shutter button halfway. That's why you do that, to give the camera a moment to focus (as well as to set exposure). That standard method of automatic focus (Auto Focus, or AF) is fine for subjects that aren't moving much. You simply need to get used to the fraction of a second delay as the camera focuses. (DSLRs don't usually have this focus delay.) Your camera may call this One Shot AF or Single Shot AF.

For subjects that are moving, you may need another form of automatic focus: Continuous Auto Focus (CAF). As the name implies, CAF constantly focuses, even when you are not pressing the shutter button. An advantage of CAF is the elimination of that brief delay for focusing, which is great for catching subjects in motion. A disadvantage of CAF is the drain on the batteries caused by the constant focusing. CAF may also have some associated noise as it constantly adjusts focus, and this may result in a modest increase in wear and tear on the mechanism.

Where in the frame to focus

But what is the camera actually focusing on? Does a camera recognize the subject of a photo? You may want to focus on that pretty bird in the tree, while the camera is automatically focusing on the twig in the foreground, blurring the bird. What determines the *focal point* (the part of the frame used to focus)? Focal point sounds too small — think of this instead as the *focus area* that the camera uses to focus.

Your camera doesn't know what the subject of the photo is. Instead, your camera is set to focus on one or more areas within the frame. Standard AF uses a relatively wide area around the center of the frame to focus. You may see this as a rectangle or brackets on your EVF or LCD. (The rectangle or brackets may turn green when the subject is in focus.)

Your camera may let you choose Center Focus (CF). With CF, the focus area is reduced to more of a square than a broad rectangle. Use CF to reduce the area the camera focuses on, such as when you want to photograph one person in a crowd.

Some cameras feature Multipoint Focus (MF), in which the camera focuses on a number of areas (determined by the manufacturer, in most cases). Some recent cameras have a variation on MF called *face detection*, as well as *smile detection*. These cameras are programmed to recognize faces and smiles. (Really!)

The distance between you and the subject

Regardless of when or where the camera is focusing, how does it know that your subject is six feet and not twenty feet away? This is another task that the brain handles subconsciously, in most cases, but cameras are programmed to calculate.

Most cameras measure distance by using some form of range-finder based on optics, infrared (especially in low light), or sound (like a bat). Lasers were used until the first few subjects vanished in a puff of smoke. (Just kidding!)

The camera's calculation of how far away the subject is can be affected by low light or objects between the lens and the subject. So, that's where Manual Focus comes in. When you choose Manual Focus, you tell your camera how far away the subject is by using left (closer) and right (farther) controls while watching a scale on-screen with distances marked up to infinity. Manual Focus takes the control away from the camera and leaves it to you to guess distances accurately. Manual Focus is not very useful for moving subjects.

Locking focus

In most cases, pressing the shutter button halfway locks the focus until you press all the way down or release the button, no matter how focus was determined by the camera. You might deliberately lock focus on a subject before moving the camera a little to one side or the other. This takes the subject out of the center of the frame but ensures that the subject is in focus. An off-center subject may be more interesting, as long as the subject is in focus.

When you want to shoot a subject off-center, lock the focus. Set the Auto Focus option to Center Focus or One Shot AF mode. If your camera has an option to select a single focus point or AF, select it. (Check your camera's user manual to find out how.)

Figure 3-1 shows an off-center subject. For this photo, the shutter button was pressed halfway down to lock the focus with the subject in the center of the frame. Then the camera was moved to create a more interesting composition.

 Locking focus on a subject can help you in situations where the camera might focus on the wrong thing. For example, when you're photographing a bird in a tree, the camera might focus on branches closer to you than the bird. To adjust for this, focus on an object the same distance from you as the bird, lock the focus, and move the camera to frame the bird. (This trick works on other subjects, too. It requires a good sense of distance.) Similarly, focusing on the space between two people might put both out of focus. Focus on one, lock the focus, and move the camera to put them both in the frame.

Photo credit: Todd Pearson/PhotoDisc

Figure 3-1: Lock the focus before you shoot an off-center subject.

Working with depth of field

No matter which mechanism your camera uses to focus — Auto Focus, Manual Focus, Center Focus, Multipoint Focus — there is always the issue of depth of field (DOF). DOF is covered in Chapter 2. You may recall that there is a range in front of the focal point (the area between the camera and the subject) and beyond or behind the subject that is in focus — that's the DOF.

Imagine three rows of volleyball players standing on bleachers. If the camera focuses on the middle row, will the players in the first and last row be in focus? They will be if there is sufficient DOF. If the DOF is shallow, the other rows will be out of focus. That may be just what you want if you like someone in the middle row.

Aperture directly affects DOF. If you are operating in any mode other than Aperture Priority, Program mode, or Manual mode, the aperture setting remains in the camera's control, along with the DOF. (See Chapter 2 if you need a refresher on how aperture affects DOF or to find out more about Program mode.) There is nothing wrong with letting the camera manage settings. When you control the aperture and DOF settings, you may create photos that are different from what the camera would do automatically. Those photos may be better, but some surely will be worse as you experiment. You have to break a lot of eggs to photograph an omelet.

 To play around with DOF, look in the early morning and late afternoon for natural spotlighting of bright objects in front of darker, shaded backgrounds.

Figure 3-2 shows an image of a coneflower with a very shallow depth of field, resulting in a blurred background.

Figure 3-3, on the other hand, shows Lily Pond in Colorado, with a very deep depth of field that results in near and far objects that look equally sharp.

Photo credit: Mark Justice Hinton

Figure 3-2: An image with a shallow depth of field.

Photo credit: Mark Justice Hinton

Figure 3-3: An image with a deep depth of field.

If you want to create a shallow depth of field, use one of the techniques from the following list:

✔ **Shoot in Portrait mode.** Look for an icon of head and shoulders. This mode sets the camera to a larger aperture.

✔ **Set your camera to Aperture Priority (A or Av) mode.** Choose a wide aperture, which, ironically, is indicated by a lower f stop number. For example, f2.8 is a larger aperture than f16. Try various aperture settings to create the DOF you're looking for. (See Chapter 2 if you need a refresher on setting the aperture.)

✔ **Use a telephoto lens and fill your frame with the subject.** The longer the focal length of your lens, the shallower the DOF.

✔ **Move close to your subject.** The closer you are, the shallower the DOF.

On most consumer and prosumer cameras, you won't really see the DOF until you look at the picture afterward. DSLRs may have a preview button that helps you see the DOF.

In you want to create a deep DOF, try one of these techniques:

✔ **Shoot in Landscape mode.** Look for the mountain icon on your camera. This mode sets the camera to a narrower aperture.

✔ **Set your camera to Aperture Priority (A or Av) mode.** Choose a narrow aperture, such as f16 or f22. Experiment with settings to create the depth of field you want.

✔ **Use a wide-angle lens to increase the impact of a deep DOF.**

✔ **Move farther away from your subject.**

Keep in mind that DOF refers to how much area is in focus in front and in back of your subject. When you want to minimize a busy, distracting background and make your subject a strong focal point, use a shallow DOF, which blurs the background. When you want the entire image (from the foreground to the background) to be sharply in focus, use a deep DOF.

Metering to evaluate scene brightness

For each photo you shoot, your camera evaluates the available light and analyzes the areas of light and dark within the frame. This analysis is called *metering* and comes from the traditional film technique that involves a hand-held or internal light meter. With a hand-held light meter, you can aim the meter at the part of the scene you want to use to determine the exposure (this is called *metering off* an object). Even though most nonprofessional camera owners won't use a hand-held meter, your camera has a built-in device that meters off all or part of the scene.

To control the exposure, especially in scenes with stark contrast between light and dark areas, consider how the camera determines the brightness of a scene. Imagine a marble statue surrounded by dark-green vegetation. If you meter off the statue, say, by moving close to it or zooming in, the camera adjusts for a bright scene and avoids overexposure. In the process, the greenery may be underexposed, which is not necessarily bad. If you meter off the greenery, either by aiming away from the statue or by backing off so that the statue is a small part of the scene, the camera adjusts for a darker scene and avoids underexposure. In the process, the statue will probably be overexposed.

All DSLRs and many prosumer cameras use various metering methods. These methods define the way the image sensor in the camera measures the light in the shot and calculates the appropriate exposure for the image.

Some of these metering methods are described in the following list:

- **Evaluative metering (also known as *matrix*, *multi-segment*, or *multi-zone* metering):** This method looks at the subject's position and brightness and the foreground, middle ground, and background lighting. Evaluative metering evaluates up to 100% of the scene and averages the lighting to determine the appropriate exposure.

  For most scenes, this is a sensible metering method, which is why evaluative metering is the standard method used by most cameras unless you choose otherwise. As you would expect, some cameras enable metering changes, and some do not.

- **Spot, or partial, metering:** This method of metering bases exposure on the light in the center of the frame (approximately 10 to 15 percent of the frame). You might choose spot metering for backlit scenes, in which the background is much brighter than the subject. Doing so causes the camera to adjust to let in more light to properly expose the backlit subject. That, in turn, may overexpose the background. If you want a silhouette, you may want to meter off the bright background to cause the camera to underexpose the subject.

- **Center-weighted metering:** This method meters off the center, giving that information *weight*

(emphasis or preference) and then meters the
rest of the scene. This isn't quite an average
because it is weighted toward the center metering, making this a cross between evaluative and
spot metering. This mode is good for complex
lighting situations.

If your camera offers metering options, take a few
minutes to explore them by following these steps:

1. **Put your camera in Manual (M) mode and press
   the Metering button or choose the setup menu.**

   Generally, this mode is indicated by an eye icon;
   check your camera's user's manual if you don't
   see that icon.

2. **Select from the available metering modes on
   the menu: evaluative (or multi), spot, or center-
   weighted. (See the descriptions in the preceding
   bullet list if you need help in choosing a mode.)**

3. **Take a few different shots from the same spot,
   looking for a variety of light and contrast.**

4. **Without moving from that spot, switch metering
   methods and take the same shots.**

 The various effects you get from different metering methods can be very subtle on your camera's LCD. To really tell the difference among
images, you need to transfer the photos to your
computer and compare them on that screen.

Composing the Photograph

So far, we've had you pretty fixated on technology —
simply nailing down how to find and select the right
setting for a particular shot. In this section, we help

you snap up some technique (okay, bad pun). People have been taking and viewing photographs for ages, and you get to benefit from all they've learned.

The concept of *point-and-shoot* belies the amount of thought that precedes good *composition*, which is the conscious arrangement of elements in a scene. Along with juggling various mechanical settings — or using Automatic mode — consider improving the composition of your photograph by incorporating the suggestions discussed in this section. You find out how to place and enhance the subject, how to minimize distractions, and some ways to develop a particular mood for a shot. You may also see some photos that defy guidelines but are interesting, nonetheless.

Finding a focal point

If a photo contains too many elements, the eye doesn't know where to look first. Beware the wandering eye. A focal point draws your viewer to a main point of interest within the image. One of the easiest compositional tasks is to find a clearly defined focal point.

Consider a city street corner with a lot of traffic signs, a couple of billboards, and dozens of people moving in every direction. That chaos might actually be the subject of a photo. But if the actual subject is a dog sitting by a lamppost, people looking at the photo may miss that point. (The *Where's Waldo?* series proves people enjoy hunting for the subject under some circumstances.)

A clear focal point should include only necessary elements that contribute to the compositional strength or emotional impact of your image, eliminating distractions. Here are a couple of suggestions:

✔ If you're photographing people or animals, try to get close to them by moving or using a zoom lens. (Using the zoom allows for more candid photos.)

✔ If you're shooting open scenes, find something interesting to include in the frame. Shots of mountains and beaches are fine, but how many are truly memorable? Throw in a climber scaling the mountain wall or a surfer wiping out on a wave and you elevate the visual impact to another level.

 Elements that distract from your focal point, and which you should try to avoid, include too much background and random clutter and bystanders.

Figure 3-4 shows an off-center focal point (a sunflower seedling) emphasized by natural lighting.

Photo credit: Mark Justice Hinton

Figure 3-4: The focal point can be anywhere in the frame.

Every guideline has exceptions. A field of flowers may not have a focal point but may smell as sweet.

Reducing background clutter

Most people worry only about cutting off people's heads when they shoot. (Now that's a gruesome sentence!) However, a bigger problem is that most people include too many elements in their shots, distracting from the focal point. Try to eliminate background clutter that adds nothing to the value of your shot.

Here are a few tips for reducing unnecessary elements in your photo compositions:

- ✔ **Get close.** Fill your frame with your subject.

- ✔ **Move your camera, yourself, or your subject.** Try shooting a vertical or diagonal shot if the subject warrants it. If moving your camera isn't enough, move around your subject and try unexpected angles. Look for compositions that minimize or avoid distracting elements around your subject, such as poles, wires, fences, or bright lights.

- ✔ **Include only complementary background elements.** If your background elements are interesting and give context to your subject, include them. These elements can include props, landmarks, and natural components.

- ✔ **Try blurring an unavoidable, undesirable background.** Sometimes you can do this by using a wider aperture on your camera, such as f4 instead of f11 or f16. This strategy makes the depth of field shallower so that your subject is sharp but the background isn't. Keep in mind that some consumer digital cameras use image sensors that are about one-third the size of a 35mm frame, making the lens close to the sensor, which increases the depth of field. This type of sensor can make it hard to blur the background. You can always blur the background by applying a blur filter during editing.

 You can move around your subject, choosing the least distracting or most interesting background for your shot.

Following the Rule of Thirds

Very few photographic guidelines have been elevated to the status of a *rule*, but this section tells you about one of them. The Rule of Thirds divides the photo into horizontal thirds, vertical thirds, or a grid of nine squares (3 x 3).

For a very simple example of the effect of thirds, stand where you can see the horizon. Looking through the VF or using the LCD, position the horizon one third up from the bottom of the frame. Shoot or take a mental picture. Move the camera slightly to position the horizon two-thirds up from the bottom. Which of these pictures is better depends on your intent and the subject. Either may be better than dividing the frame in half with the horizon.

Figure 3-5 shows a photo of a kayaker overlaid with a grid. The Rule of Thirds suggests that the focal point should be at or near one of the four intersections around the middle of the picture, along one of the thirds — vertical, horizontal, or both. Placing the subject or focal point along the thirds makes it more likely to be noticed first and, some say, is subconsciously more pleasing.

Photo credit: Corbis Digital Stock

Figure 3-5: Position your subject by using the Rule of Thirds.

Regarding Figure 3-5, you could argue that the center of the kayaker's body should be on the closest intersection point. The bottom horizontal gridline could run through the paddle, the kayak (lower) or the line in the water (lower still). Each adjustment would be a different photograph. All might be better than the kayaker in the center of the frame. Remember, the Rule of Thirds is only a guideline.

To apply the Rule of Thirds to various shots, consider these examples:

✔ **In a scenic shot:** A low horizon creates a spacious feeling; a high horizon gives an intimate feeling.

✔ **In a portrait:** Try putting the face or eyes of the person along a vertical or horizontal third or at one of the four points of intersection.

If you have a camera with Auto Focus, lock the focus when you're moving from center because the Auto Focus sensor locks on to whatever is in the center of the viewfinder (unless you've manually chosen a different focus method). Center your subject in the viewfinder and apply slight pressure to the shutter release button to lock the focus. Then reposition your subject at an intersecting point and press the shutter release the rest of the way to take the photo.

Even the mighty Rule of Thirds has exceptions. You may choose to put your subject dead center, knowing that you expect to crop the picture later, either filling the frame with the subject or cropping with the subject off-center (and, more than likely, along one of the thirds).

Avoiding mergers

As you intently frame and compose your photo, you might fail to see a branch in the background that will seem to grow out of your friend's ear in the final photo. Such a gaffe is called a *merger*. Or, you might not notice that you're chopping off someone's hand or foot. This is known as a *border merger*.

Effects like these are common and amusing and, with luck, not too embarrassing. You can avoid mergers by thoroughly scanning the preview in the EVF or LCD and thinking about the background and foreground as much as you do about the subject. You may be able to avoid a problem with the background by moving your position or by reducing the depth of field (widening the aperture with a lower f stop).

Figure 3-6 shows a border merger attacking a cheetah.

Photo credit: Corbis Digital Stock

Figure 3-6: Avoid border mergers.

 With the best photo editing software and enough time, it's easier to brush away a branch than to restore a severed limb.

Looking for balance

You create balance in an image through the arrangement or placement of the elements in the image. Balance can be *symmetrical* (harmonious or formal) or *asymmetrical* (dynamic or informal). Think of balance in regard to color, shape, and contrast.

Imagine two photographs of a chessboard. In the first, all the pieces are lined up before the game begins. Shot from above or from the level of the board, the scene has a natural symmetry and balance among the pieces.

Now, the game is over. In a corner, two pieces stand over the fallen king — checkmate! The unbalanced image is part of the story.

Figure 3-7 shows a balanced rock, or *hoodoo,* as an example of asymmetrical balance — that rock will fall in a century or so. In this case, the subject itself is dynamic (if only in geologic time) and tense. Notice, as well, the rough thirds described by the foreground, the mountains, and the sky. The balancing rock is also along one vertical third, tipping over one of the four intersections. The stark contrast on the two sides of the spire is another element of balance.

Photo credit: PhotoDisc

Figure 3-7: Asymmetrical balance creates tension and implies impending motion.

Finding leading lines

With some photos, your eye wanders haphazardly across the image, which isn't necessarily a bad thing. However, you may want to compose a stronger picture that leads the eye purposefully across the image.

Leading lines draw the eye into the picture. They add dimension and depth and can be actual lines or lines implied by the composition of elements.

To compose photos with leading lines, look for elements such as roads, fences, rivers, and bridges. Diagonal lines are dynamic. Curved lines are harmonious. Horizontal lines are peaceful. Vertical lines are active — or so some people say. Regardless of emotive quality, a line leads the eye.

The line of clouds in this photo of Chaco Canyon, New Mexico, shown in Figure 3-8, demonstrates how a leading line can direct your eye across an image. In Figure 3-8, the horizon (along the lower third) doesn't draw the eye left or right. The clouds lead the eye toward the lower right — and there's Waldo! This print may be too small for you to see the photographer's shadow in the lower-right corner. Such a shadow is generally regarded as a mistake. Here, it was intentional.

Keeping the horizon straight

For some reason, people expect horizons to be horizontal. (That must have something to do with the real world.) You can spoil a dramatic sunrise or sunset by too much tilt to the left or right. Try to keep a straight head on your shoulders or learn to compensate for your natural inclinations.

Photo credit: Mark Justice Hinton

Figure 3-8: Leading lines (the clouds, in this case) bring the eye into and across the image.

Figure 3-9 shows a flat, straight horizon. What rule does this figure violate? *Hint:* It's the only rule in this chapter. The Rule of Thirds suggests moving the horizon up as much again as you see here, showing more of the foreground. Would that be a better shot? Following rules doesn't guarantee anything.

If your camera has a viewfinder screen with a built-in grid for the purpose of helping you keep the horizon straight, use it. Alternatively, you can purchase a bubble-level accessory to let you know whether your camera is tilted.

Using a tripod can also help keep your horizons straight. And some tripods come with built-in bubble levels. Just make sure that the legs of your tripod are extended properly — equally on level ground, or lopsidedly on uneven ground — to make the camera level. (You can read more about using a tripod in Chapter 2.)

Photo credit: Corbis Digital Stock

Figure 3-9: Keep horizons straight.

 Keep in mind that once you know the rules, you can always break them. But it's much more fun to break the rules you know than to operate out of ignorance.

Framing the subject

The term *frame* is used to describe the image itself. You frame your subject, and the lines in the composition, such as the horizon or roads — as well as movement — extend beyond the frame. Inside this frame, you can further frame the subject by including elements around the foreground that surround the subject. Imagine a lake appearing flanked by trees or a shot through a doorway or window looking inside or looking outside.

Figure 3-10 shows a doorway in Chaco Canyon framing part of a room beyond within the frame of the photo. The doorway in this photo may violate the Rule of Thirds because the right edge cuts the scene in half, unless you imagine the left-hand vertical third down the middle of the doorway. Showing more of the wall to the right would be more in line with the Rule of Thirds (one-third doorway, two-thirds wall).

Here are a few more points to keep in mind about framing within a photo:

- ✔ **A frame welcomes you to an image, adds depth, and creates a point of reference.**

- ✔ **To compose photos with frames, use foreground elements to frame your subjects.** Elements such as tree branches, windows, and doorways can frame wide or long shots. Close-up shots can also be framed.

Photo credit: Mark Justice Hinton

Figure 3-10: It can be fun to put frames within frames.

> ✔ **Decide whether to keep your framing elements
> sharply focused or soft.** Depending on the shot,
> sometimes sharply focused framing elements
> can distract from, rather than enhance, the focal
> point.

Creating a mood with distance

A memorable photograph often creates or conveys a
mood. The subject is clearly significant, but light and
distance also impart a mood.

Getting close to your subject may make the image
personal, warm, and inviting. Avoid including exces-
sive background elements, and intimately fill your
frame with your subject, especially when photographing people.

Figure 3-11 shows the subject's joy in an odd find on
the trail (a gastrolith). This photo illustrates the intimacy that comes with getting close to your subject.

You might even violate guidelines for framing
and against mergers by getting exaggeratedly
close to your subject. A close-up of a face, even
just eyes, nose, and mouth, can be very interesting. A good zoom lens allows you to get especially close without aggravating your subject.

And just as shooting close can create a feeling of intimacy, shooting a subject with a lot of space around it
can evoke a sense of loneliness or isolation. It all
depends on your intended message.

Use eye contact when photographing people.
Remember that children, animals, and other
height-challenged subjects aren't at the same
eye level as adults. Try getting down on the
ground, to their level, if necessary.

Photo credit: Mark Justice Hinton

Figure 3-11: Getting close to your subject affects the mood of the picture.

Using texture and shape

When composing your shot, look for interesting textures to add definition and for lines and shapes to create interest. Remember that textures and shapes are enhanced by the use of light and shadow. These elements come into play even more when you're shooting black-and-white images.

Figure 3-12 shows the effect of texture in an image. This photo of a rock wall in Chetro Ketl, New Mexico, emphasizes the natural texture of the stone plus the sculptural quality of the mason's work. This photo might be even more interesting in black and white.

Photo credit: Mark Justice Hinton

Figure 3-12: Using texture for added definition.

Check your camera's settings or refer to your user's guide to see whether your camera offers a black-and-white (B&W) setting. Alternatively, you can switch from color to B&W during editing.

Chapter 4

Photographing Special Subjects

In This Chapter

▶ Photographing people

▶ Capturing animals

▶ Recording special events

▶ Shooting outdoors under various conditions

*E*very photographer has a favorite or special sub-ject. You may like zoos, or you may be the one your friends expect to photograph their wedding. The land, sky, or water may be your thing.

Beyond the general guidelines and principles of pho-tography (see Chapters 2 and 3), you'll find that spe-cial subjects warrant special handling. A wedding is not a zoo, no matter how it feels on that special day. Birthday parties and rainy landscapes require differ-ent plans — such as how to wipe icing versus mud off the camera.

In this chapter, you consider people, animals, events, and places as subjects presenting unique challenges and opportunities. Of course, these topics can overlap — you can get married at the zoo in a rain-storm. Now those would be some pictures!

The advantage of digital photography is that you don't have to worry about the cost and time spent in film processing, so you can let your experimental and creative juices flow and take lots of pictures without worry or guilt. Just be sure to spend enough time with your camera before the big day to avoid unpleasant surprises. ("What lens cap?")

Capturing People and Animals

Most people love looking at people and other animals. There are countless ways to photograph the creatures we encounter at home, around town, and in the wild.

Everybody loves a picture of a grinning human baby, a cuddly kitty, or a playful puppy — well, maybe not everybody, but you may not want to know anyone who hates all three. And don't leave out birds and bugs — or plants, for that matter — all can capture the heart and imagination.

The best photographs tell a story or convey a mood. A photo can cause us to share even a stranger's joy or sorrow, draw a breath at the sight of some lovely creature, or recall or imagine what it was like the day that photo was taken.

Photographs freeze a moment or an aspect of life. You may cringe at the sight years later; but more likely, everyone will delight in seeing how things used to be.

Taking a portrait

A portrait of one or two people can be very formal or casual. The subject of a portrait can fill the image or be framed by the immediate surroundings. And you can shoot a portrait in either portrait or landscape orientation.

The best portraits do more than merely capture an instant in a person's life — they reveal something unique or memorable about that person in that captured moment.

Don't worry about creating *art* — a candid snapshot can become a treasured keepsake. But if time and circumstance allow, invest some thought in the composition. Figure 4-1 shows a candid portrait of a subject absorbed by what he is seeing.

Photo credit: Mark Justice Hinton

Figure 4-1: A candid portrait can become a treasured keepsake.

When you're shooting a portrait, the most important thing you can do is take care of your subject. Here are some suggestions on how to do just that:

- ✔ If possible, photograph the person in a location where she feels comfortable. Chat with her and make her feel relaxed.

- ✔ To achieve the highest level of intimacy and engagement by viewers of the portrait, go for direct eye contact — that is, have your subject looking straight toward your lens. If your subject is looking away from the camera, however (which can add mystery), decide whether you want to include any of the surroundings to show the person's point of view.

- ✔ Sunglasses and hats shading the eyes can make or spoil the shot. So think about whether you want your subject to remove them.

- ✔ Try to include some context in a portrait, which means photographing the person in surroundings that speak to who she is: her profession, hobby, or personal life. Include tools of the trade or props, if appropriate.

- ✔ If the person is posing, try to grab some candid shots when she isn't paying attention. If you're posing her, have her turn slightly to the side, angle her shoulders, and lean in slightly toward the camera. Watch out for glare on eyeglasses.

- ✔ For children, get down to their level, be patient, and take some candid shots. Let children lose their shyness in play.

With two people centered in the frame, you may have trouble focusing on them and not the background between them when you use Auto Focus. Try focusing on one person and locking the focus by pressing the shutter halfway down.

Then reposition the camera on the couple and
press the shutter the rest of the way.

After making your subject comfortable, compose your
photograph and choose your settings. Here are some
things to consider before you shoot:

- ✔ Incorporate general rules about composition
  (see Chapter 3), such as moving in close and
  using the Rule of Thirds (discussed in Chapter 3)
  for a great portrait. Place the eyes along an
  intersecting grid line and reduce background
  clutter unless it contributes to the shot in
  some way.

- ✔ Many cameras have a Portrait mode that keeps
  your subject in focus while blurring the background (look for an icon with a head). Some
  cameras also have a Portrait/Landscape setting,
  which keeps both the subject and background
  in focus (the icon may be a head in front of a triangular mountain symbol).

- ✔ Shoot a variety of shots: close-ups, medium
  shots, and even full body. Create a lot of images
  that you can choose from.

- ✔ Outside, shoot in natural light at a 45-degree
  angle to the sun. Overcast days create a soft,
  flattering light. Shooting right before sunset creates a soft, warm light. Avoid harsh midday sun
  at all costs. People squint, and the sun causes
  nasty shadows across the face.

- ✔ Inside, place people near a window, at a
  45-degree angle to the light. If you need to light
  the shadowed side of the face, place something
  reflective nearby, such as light-colored card-
  board or even a lamp (with or without a shade),
  placed at a 45-degree angle. Remember that soft
  lighting is the key with portraits. If you must use

a flash, be sure to set Red-Eye Reduction mode.
(You can also correct red-eye in editing.)

✔ Keep a low ISO (100 to 200) to minimize noise.
ISO settings refer to how sensitive the image
sensor is to light. If you're using a slow shutter,
use a tripod to ensure a sharp capture. If you're
shooting in Manual mode and not using a tripod,
set the shutter to around $\frac{1}{125}$ second.

If you're photographing someone you don't
know — for example, someone you run into
while on vacation — be sure to ask for the person's permission.

For a casual self-portrait, aim the camera toward
yourself while you hold the camera at arm's
length; then snap a picture. Use the short timer,
if you can't press the Shutter Release button at
arm's length. Don't use the zoom. With some
practice and luck, the resulting picture can be
spontaneous and fun. You can also use a mirror
or other reflective surface, like plate glass or
water, for a self-portrait, as shown in Figure 4-2.
Don't use the flash when you shoot close to
glass or mirrors — the flash will white out the
shot.

Figure 4-2: Self-portraits are fun.

Getting the group

Photographing a group takes determination and coop-
eration. Teams are easy; families can be trickier.
Don't even try to get everyone at the bus stop to pose
together.

Take all the considerations of a portrait and multiply
them by the number in a group. How many people
will have their eyes closed? Will everyone look at the
camera and smile at the same time? At the very least,
be prepared to take extra pictures.

Sometimes, taking a great group shot is a matter of
serendipity. But usually it requires direction and
setup from the photographer. Don't be afraid to play
director and tell people where and how to stand, sit,
or position themselves. Just be considerate of people's time and don't make them wait too long.

Find the best location and, if possible, use props such
as viewing stands, steps, picnic tables, trees, or other
elements to arrange people.

After you scout and set up the location, position
people in a variety of poses. Depending on the
number of people, having some sit or kneel in front
and others stand in back can work well. Stagger
people in front and behind.

Having people get close, tilting their heads toward
each other and even touching one another, often
makes the shot more intimate and engaging. Figure
4-3 shows a group barely squeezed into a tent.

Photo credit: Mark Justice Hinton

Figure 4-3: Direct people how to fit within the frame.

 You can join the group by setting up the shot on a tripod and using the self-timer. Let everyone know what position you'll take when you join the group and make sure you'll fit in the frame. Make everyone hold positions until you check the photo.

If you have an especially large group of people or active kids or pets, ask for a volunteer to help with the directing. And when photographing really large groups, if you move higher and focus down on the group, you can squeeze more people into the frame.

If a group of people is engaged in an activity, like a game, bring elements of the location or activity into the shot to give the photo context.

Finally, after you set up the shot, try to get people to relax. Use humor to get people to smile naturally. It's the next best thing to spontaneity.

Capturing animals in the shot

Wild or tame, animals touch us all in some way. Some photos of animals can be staged, as you can stage portraits of humans. Your dog may sit on command. Your cat may ignore you and refuse to move out of the frame. The hamster's got no place to go on that wheel.

Figure 4-4 shows a portrait of a contemplative pet cat.

Unless you are trying to take a photo of a pet rock or a Tamagochi, be ready for unexpected movement. Take multiple shots in close, and then move back and take some more. (Move in and out physically or with a zoom lens. Keep in mind that zooming in usually reduces the depth of field.)

Photo credit: Mark Justice Hinton

Figure 4-4: Animal portraits can be as engaging as those of humans.

Spontaneous animal photos involve more luck with the timing. The first step with any spontaneous photo is to always have your camera ready. That means the lens cap is off and the camera is on anytime you might luck into a photo. You may even want to keep your hand on the trigger. This is the price of your art: eternal vigilance.

Figure 4-5 shows a flock of snow geese taking off. Be ready for the unexpected movement of animals.

Photo credit: Mark Justice Hinton

Figure 4-5: Spontaneity happens, although some animal movements are predictable.

To conserve battery power, your camera shuts down after a preset idle period. Using the set-up menus, you may be able to make the idle period longer for readiness at the expense of power. You can also half-press the shutter periodically to keep the power on.

You can also improve your chances of getting a good, spontaneous shot by observing animal behavior. What part of the fence do the birds favor? In which direction is that animal likely to move? Will it pause for a second? (It might, if you don't alarm it. Animals are curious, too.) When you know which way the butterfly will turn, you've reached *nerdvana*.

If possible, move the camera down to the animal's level. For an intimate photo, capture the animal closely and at eye level. If you can't get close physically, use a zoom lens. Get your pet's attention by holding a treat or toy next to the camera.

Photograph the animal in a location it likes so that the animal is relaxed and feels comfortable. A location that provides context adds to the ambience of the photo. A source of water usually draws wildlife.

Try to capture the animal's personality and charm. Is your dog a live wire? Is your cat the ultimate couch potato? Is that skunk a little stinker? Whatever its personality, try to capture the special trait that defines the animal. And, as with portraits of people, often the candid, rather than posed, shot is the best. (And don't even think about posing that skunk.)

Be careful using a flash when photographing an animal. The flash may make the animal uncomfortable and even scare it. Try to capture the animal in natural light, if possible. Interestingly, whereas shots of people may incur red-eye from a flash, shots of animals usually incur *green-eye*, which may be harder to remove in editing.

If the animal you're photographing has very dark or very light fur, you may need to slightly underexpose or overexpose the shot, respectively, to retain detail in the fur.

Similarly to the process you use when photographing an athlete, you may need to shoot with a fast shutter speed (check your camera's Manual mode capability) or in Sports mode, which selects a fast shutter for you.

 Many cameras have a Continuous, or Burst, mode. In Burst mode, the camera takes multiple photos while you hold down the shutter button. Cameras differ in how many photos are taken and the amount of time between photos. For subjects that move, especially animals and people at play, you're almost certain to capture at least one photo you like from the series. Burst mode may be wasted on a subject that isn't moving, although you may capture an important but subtle change in the subject.

 If you're shooting through glass at home, at the zoo, or from your car, find a clean spot and get as close to the glass as you can. To eliminate reflections, some cameras have a lens hood that extends a couple of inches beyond the lens. And, if it's available, include some natural surroundings with the animal to give the photo context.

Bag birds in the backyard

Birds are beautiful subjects, especially if you can catch one in a close-up. Because birds are almost constantly in motion, though, you may want to create a setting that encourages them to gather and linger. For example, you could try any of the following:

✔ If you have the time and means, create habitat. Plant trees and shrubs, especially those that bear fruit or seeds that birds eat or that provide places for birds to perch, hide, and nest. Figure 4-6 shows a robin carrying nesting material.

Figure 4-6: Attract birds to your backyard by providing a safe haven.

- ✔ Hang bird feeders, suet, and seed bells close enough to windows that you can get really close with a zoom lens but not so close that you scare away birds when you stand at the window. Most cameras focus through relatively clean glass. If the glass is dirty enough, or if you're shooting through screen, the camera may focus on the wrong spot.

- ✔ Put perches, such as lattice, near food to encourage birds to sit and pose.

- ✔ Put water in a shallow, wide pan. Birds will drink and some will bathe. (Robins love to bathe.) Add water every day and clean the bath at least once per week. Add a bird bath heating element to your water source in winter.

✔ Use Burst mode to take several shots in rapid succession to catch birds in different positions.

✔ Park a comfortable chair near a window with your camera, binoculars, and a bird book nearby. Or look outside every time you pass a window.

Pointers for photographing animals

Animals are great photographic subjects. Many of us share our lives with dogs, cats, and other pets. Depending on where you live or travel, you may encounter less-domesticated animals, from livestock to the truly wild. Here are some points to consider when photographing animals:

✔ **Turn off your flash.** The burst of light is likely to frighten an animal.

✔ **Use your camera's Action or Sports mode.** Using these modes increases your chances of catching animals in motion.

✔ **Photograph your furry friends.** You'll never tire of these photos (although your human friends may have limits). Catch your pet in a character-istic pose or maybe something a little unusual (like the time my dog, Lucky, tried to climb a tree).

✔ **Go where the animals are.** That may be your own backyard or a neighborhood park, or it may mean venturing out into fields and forests. Figure 4-7 shows elk foraging. (Okay, I admit: I snapped that from pavement.) A reliable water source, such as a stream or lake, usually attracts wildlife throughout the day and night.

Figure 4-7: Keep a safe distance from wildlife of any kind.

✔ **Stay safe.** Rangers in Yellowstone National Park tell of parents smearing peanut butter on a child's face to get a cute picture of a bear licking the child. Need I say it? Don't do that! Keep some distance from all wild creatures for their safety, as well as your own. Use a **zoom lens** to get closer. (Wildlife photography benefits from using an ultrazoom of 12X or greater.)

✔ **Fake it.** Go to a zoo. Use a zoom lens to get in close and to hide cages and bars. Photograph animals watching people watching animals or vice versa. Most of us will never get closer to lions and tigers and bears.

Documenting Events

From time to time, you may find yourself taking photos in a structured, organized, or more constrained setting, such as a sporting event, wedding, or group meal. The good thing about shooting a scheduled event is that you know in advance when and where people will be and what they are likely to be doing at a given moment.

The challenge of taking photos for an event, of course, is that most events restrict your movement and your freedom to use a flash or yell "Stop!" Think about the event ahead of time and recall similar events and the photos you took or have seen from these events. Plan ahead and remain flexible — remember, the unplanned photo is very often the most interesting.

During an event is not the time to wonder how a particular camera mode works or "what was the difference between aperture and shutter speed?" Do your homework and come prepared. Have lots of space on your memory card (or take spares) and some extra batteries. Practice changing batteries or cards as quickly as you can. You want to be free to think about composition, not mechanics.

Games, sports, or other events with quick action require specific preparation. Weddings, on the other hand, tend to unfold at a much slower pace. But remember that neither event offers the chance to pause or redo.

Freezing action

One of the great benefits of digital *video* cameras is that you can relive every minute of a game or other event. Usually, there are moments that stand out above all the rest. In those moments may be found the best photos of the event.

How do you capture the bat meeting the ball, the goal, or the spike with a regular digital camera, however? With preparation, a fast shutter speed, and some luck.

 Most cameras have a Sports mode that increases the shutter speed and adjusts all other settings automatically. (Look for an icon of a golfer, a runner, or a ball.) Take advantage of Sports mode and remember it in other circumstances that require quick captures (such as photographing wildlife).

Here are some things to consider when you want to freeze the action in a shot:

- ✓ **Have a plan.** Know in advance what kinds of shots you want to get. Of course, being familiar with the event or sport helps you determine which shots would be most interesting to capture.

- ✓ **Position yourself in the best location to capture the action.** This location may vary as the game, activity, or time of day progresses. In general, keep the sun at your back.

- ✓ **Use a telephoto or zoom lens to help you get close to the action.**

 A monopod (similar to a tripod, but with only one leg) is extremely useful when you're using long, heavy lenses. It's lightweight and almost as steady as a tripod, but you can move it easily to chase action subjects.

✔ **Be in the right place at the right time.**
Sometimes, timing is so critical that capturing
that excellent shot means pushing the shutter
just before the perfect moment. Take into
account any delay between click and capture
(*shutter lag*) your camera has.

✔ **Be aware of the background and elements
around your focal point.** Unless they add context, keep them simple and nondistracting.

✔ **For most sports, shoot at a fast shutter speed
(¹⁄₅₀₀ second or faster).** Set your camera to
Shutter Priority mode so that if the light
changes, the shutter speed stays the same and
the aperture adjusts accordingly.

Figure 4-8 shows a frozen instant, full of the action of
the game.

Remember that some events don't allow you to use a
flash. When you're shooting in low light without a
flash, try moving to a higher ISO setting. Just be
aware that this may add noise to your images.

Photo credit: Corbis Digital Stock

Figure 4-8: Be aware and capture the perfect moment.

When you're trying to keep up with a player on the move, give these settings and techniques a try:

- ✔ **Set your camera to continuous Auto Focus mode.** This mode gives you better capability to track a moving player.

- ✔ **Conversely, try Manual Focus mode.** Auto Focus may be fine for the subject you're capturing, but becoming comfortable with Manual Focus can help you get a shot when Auto Focus falls short.

- ✔ **Keep the camera on the player and adjust the focus continuously (called** _follow focus_**).**

- ✔ **Anticipate and focus on the area you expect the action to move into (the** _zone focus_**).**

- ✔ **Try panning.** Using a slower shutter speed, follow the action and press the shutter while still moving the camera. The moving subject remains in focus as other objects blur. This technique creates the illusion of movement in a photo.

Figure 4-9 shows skaters catching some air. (Do the buildings add or detract from the photo?)

 Don't forget to take some shots of the event preparations, the sidelines, the crowd, individual spectators caught up in the excitement, and the aftermath. Sometimes the most interesting and poignant shots aren't even part of the official action.

Photo credit: Corbis Digital Stock

Figure 4-9: Use zone focus and shoot where the action will be.

Photographing a birthday, graduation, or wedding

Many events that you attend are highly structured and choreographed, with multiple players performing scripts as beaming witnesses look on, often through tears of joy. These events mark transitions in people's lives, from youth to old age, from school to real life, from two into one. We want to preserve and treasure these moments forever.

But don't let the pressure of the special day get to you. Plan, prepare, know your camera, and stay flexible and alert to the moment. Be prepared with charged batteries, memory cards, and other equipment, such as lenses and a tripod, ready to rumble.

Plan some of your pictures in advance. Know when special moments will happen — blowing out candles on a cake, handing out diplomas, the big kiss. Remember that sometimes the best shots are the candid ones — someone adjusting a formal outfit, a friend or family member radiating pride, or someone goofing off. Keep in mind that discretion is the key at a formal event. No one wants to be haunted by some misbehavior caught on camera.

Scout out the best locations and vantage points for your photos. Minimize the distraction you create for participants and guests. Stay out of the way — and out of the frame — of other photographers, if possible.

Shoot a few throwaway shots to test the lighting. Use a flash only if it's allowed. If it is, consider using a flash diffuser to soften the light. If flash isn't allowed, open the aperture to a wide setting.

Remember the relevant tips in Chapter 3, such as getting in close, eliminating background clutter, composing with the Rule of Thirds, shooting at angles, and finding the light. (Also refer to the section "Getting the group," earlier in this chapter.)

Figure 4-10 shows a candid scene of two people lighting candles on a birthday cake.

Taking in food

Although we often wolf down food at the sink, at our desk, or in the car, a meal shared with others can be an event in itself. And most events feature food and drink. Food can be beautiful by its nature or its preparation. The satisfaction we experience from good food in good company can be the subject of good photographs.

You may want to photograph the food itself, the preparation, presentation and service, or the diners (with permission, of course).

When photographing food, consider the following:

- **Take time to set up a pleasing composition.** Think of the food in terms of color, shape, texture, line, and so on. If you have time and are involved with the preparation, set up alternative arrangements for your shot.

- **Use simple props.** When appropriate, props can help "set the stage" and give context to the food. Think of your setup as a still life.

- **Shoot it quickly.** Capturing food is all about getting the shot before the food starts to deteriorate or change temperature.

Photo credit: Mark Justice Hinton

Figure 4-10: Anticipate candid moments.

> ✔ **Get close to the food and shoot at plate level or higher.** One technique you may want to try is to shoot with a Macro mode or special macro lens, focusing on one part of the dish and letting the surrounding elements blur. This technique provides a strong focal point while still maintaining the context.

Figure 4-11 emphasizes the dish but provides the larger context of breakfast.

Photo credit: Digital Vision

Figure 4-11: Use simple props to give food context.

Figure 4-12 uses a macro lens to emphasize the moment of celebration. Eat, drink, and be merry.

 Food stylists all have their secret tips for making food look great. You hear stories about using shaving cream instead of whipped cream, airbrushing food with paint, and so on. Additional appetizing tips are to brush vegetable oil on food to make it glisten and to spray water on bottles to make them look wet and cold.

Photo credit: Merri Rudd

Figure 4-12: A macro lens is used here to emphasize the champagne.

Picturing Land, Sky, and Sea

Few subjects are larger than the earth. We are tiny on the landscape and in the face of the extremes of weather. The environment is a subject of great power, impact — even threat — as well as stunning beauty.

The scale of the land, sky, and sea, and the quick changeability of the weather bring different challenges and opportunities to a photographer. Too often we race over the land, not even turning our faces toward the sun, wind, rain, or land around us. A key to photographing landscapes is to stop and be there in that place.

The great outdoors — and this includes urban settings — invites a sensitivity to scale and distance. Be ready for nighttime and bad weather, as either a subject or a challenge.

Shooting landscapes and vistas

Landscapes, including the sky and bodies of water, are great subjects for photography. One challenge is conveying great distance and space in the small frame of most photographs. In your landscapes, be sure to include objects with familiar scale — animals, people, dwellings, or vehicles. You can enhance the depth of the seemingly infinite sky, for example, by including clouds, mountains, or even skyscrapers in your shot. Similarly, the vast sea might be only a puddle until you include a ship or a surfer.

Figure 4-13 uses a person to convey the scale of the scene. In this scene from Seedskadee, along the Green River in Wyoming (the name of the wildlife refuge alone makes it worth photographing), note the leading lines drawing the eye from the lower left to the center right.)

Photo credit: Mark Justice Hinton

Figure 4-13: Include people, animals, or other recognizable objects for scale in vast scenes.

Composition is the element that separates a memorable landscape shot from a mundane one. Check out the composition tips in Chapter 3, which explain how to use a focal point, the Rule of Thirds, framing, and leading lines. In that chapter, you also find out the basics of including a foreground, middle ground, and background, and shooting from different angles.

To capture expansive vistas, a wide-angle lens serves you well. A zoom lens is a wide-angle lens when it's not extended. As you zoom toward telephoto, you sacrifice width and depth for the sake of getting close to the subject. For example, if you take two shots of a mountain peak — one using a wide-angle and the other zoomed in tight — each type of photo will show something different. Likewise for a photo of someone on the beach: The wide-angle version is very different "zoomed out," showing the context; its opposite, the telephoto shot, is zoomed in emphasizing a part of the whole.

If one shot can't take in the entire scene — or, if you want a 360-degree view — try capturing the scene in several shots and then stitching them together later using a photo editor's Panorama feature. Some cameras also come with software to assist you in creating panoramas.

Here are a few more ideas to keep in mind for shooting scenery:

- ✔ **Go for the maximum depth of field (see Chapters 2 and 3).** Use a small aperture setting and a slower shutter speed (unless you're working in very bright daylight). Note that many cameras have a Landscape mode that will set up your shot for maximum depth of field and set shutter speed automatically. Keep a low ISO setting for noise-free images. (As mentioned earlier in the chapter, ISO settings refer to how sensitive the image sensor is to light.)

- ✔ **Use a tripod and self-timer or shutter release for the sharpest image.**

- ✔ **If you're shooting water, include reflections of landscape features, animals, or people.** Moving in relation to the reflections may enhance them.

- ✔ **Shooting at dawn (and immediately afterward) and dusk (and just before) gives you soft, warm lighting.** Stormy skies make dramatic backdrops. If you have a boring sky, try a polarizing filter on a DSLR for added color and contrast, or keep the horizon line high to minimize the amount of sky in the shot.

The photo of a sunset in Figure 4-14 (taken at the Bosque del Apache National Wildlife Refuge in New Mexico) uses the setting sun reflected in water to create contrast and bathe the scene in warm color.

Photo credit: Mark Justice Hinton

Figure 4-14: Dusk provides warm, soft, yet dramatic lighting on any object, including water.

Working at night

Taking photos at night requires special settings to increase the aperture (letting in more light at one time), reduce the shutter speed (giving more time for exposure), and, possibly, increase the ISO (providing more sensitivity to exposure). Your camera may handle these settings effectively with a Night Sky mode (look for a crescent moon or star symbol). You may choose to alter any or all of these settings manually.

You can change one setting manually and allow the camera to adjust the others by using Shutter Priority or Aperture Priority. You can change multiple settings with Program mode or Manual mode.

Figure 4-15 shows a tent in the dark. The slow shutter speed allows time for sparks to trace lines.

Photo credit: Corbis Digital Stock

Figure 4-15: Night shots usually require a slower shutter speed and a tripod.

You may also need to set the focus manually if the light is too low for Auto Focus to work. To shoot the sky or horizon, set the focus to Infinity.

When you're shooting at night, the camera needs a bigger, more open aperture (at least f2.8), reducing the depth of field. The shutter needs to stay open longer (⅟₃₀ second or longer). Recall that objects in motion are more likely to blur at slower shutter speeds. If you want to use a faster shutter speed, increase the ISO setting. Just keep in mind that the higher the ISO, the more *noise* your image may contain, lessening the sharpness of the image.

To ensure the best night shots, you definitely need a tripod because you need a longer exposure. Use a self-timer so that pressing the shutter button doesn't cause shakiness in your image.

 Remember that a flash helps only if your subject is directly in front of you and within range (typically 3 to 12 feet).

Start shooting before dark. Try taking shots at dusk or soon after. Capturing neon lighting is especially nice before it gets really dark and a little natural light is left.

In Figure 4-16, a little extra light shows the neon in context.

Photo credit: Corbis Digital Stock

Figure 4-16: Shoot neon lights before the evening gets pitch black to show the context.

Weathering the storm

Stormy weather might ruin your vacation or it might give you unusual and dramatic photographs. Even if rough weather doesn't inspire you, it shouldn't inhibit you if you need to get a particular shot.

Take advantage of bad weather's creative benefits. Clouds diffuse the light and eliminate harsh shadows, making for nice landscapes and even portraits. Stormy skies create dramatic backdrops for landscape shots or singular objects, such as trees or barns. Rain enhances colors and adds texture and reflections on surfaces. If the scene is gray, include a spot of color. Dark objects and colors against white create exaggerated contrast.

Figure 4-17 shows a hiker in a storm in Conejos, Colorado. The hail may not be visible in a smaller print, but the light, the rain gear, and the hiker's posture speak volumes.

Bad weather usually means less light. Make sure that your camera is capable of having a wider aperture, longer shutter speed, or both. A tripod keeps images sharp, especially for longer exposures. A self-timer can also be handy. In extremely cold weather, keep a spare battery or two warm in your pocket. Cold weather zaps battery life.

Your camera may have an option to bracket shots. This means that when you take one photo, the camera will take several, each with settings one step up or down from the settings you choose. Bracketing increases the odds that you'll get a photo under difficult exposure conditions.

Photo credit: Mark Justice Hinton

Figure 4-17: Life isn't all sunny. Harsh conditions highlight strength and drama.

Snow and fog may confuse your camera's light meter, so play it safe and bracket your shots. If your camera has a Snow mode, use it and play with shutter speeds to capture falling rain or snow.

While you're at it, though, be sure to protect your equipment. Keep your camera as dry as possible by tucking it inside your coat or shirt when you aren't shooting. Keep a soft, scratch-free cloth in your pocket to wipe off any water that gets on the camera. Going from extreme cold into a very warm environment can cause condensation to form in your equipment, so allow your equipment to warm up gradually under your coat; then, put it in a camera bag before you enter a warm room. Finally, make sure all your equipment is dry before you put it away.

Chapter 5

Taking Photos of Places and Scenery

*W*e are small upon the face of the Earth. We move through landscapes that often overwhelm the human scale. The land, sky, and sea are immense subjects that warrant special effort to capture in photographs.

Occasionally, the creations of humans rise to a truly large scale: the pyramids of Egypt and the Americas, the Great Wall of China, our best and worst cities — all of which are big challenges to photograph well.

A hallmark of landscape photos is sharp focus throughout, from near to far. Sharp focus comes naturally when the subject (the *focal point*) is far away, especially in a bright scene. If the day is cloudy or the subject is close, you may have more work to develop deep focus.

Enabling Settings for Scenery

Before you shoot pictures of landscapes and other large areas, check the following settings on your camera:

✔ **Landscape mode:** Of course, Landscape mode is a good choice when composing landscape photos. This mode sets the camera to optimize exposure in the entire frame. Take a few shots in Automatic mode for comparison.

Don't use Portrait mode for landscapes. Portrait mode tends to blur some part of the scene. For most landscapes, you want every part of the picture sharp. However, your camera may have a mode that combines Landscape and Portrait modes for photos of people in front of vistas.

✔ **Beach, Snow, and Night Sky modes:** These modes, which are suited for shooting large areas, adjust the camera for difficult exposures (too bright or too dark). Figure 5-1 shows sample camera settings. For the camera shown in the figure, I select Scene mode (the label SCN on the mode dial of this camera does not appear in the figure). Then, I use the Menu button for these settings: Twilight, Beach, Snow, and Fireworks (from left to right). More scenes are available if you scroll with the right arrow on the menu dial.

Specify scene: Night, Beach, Snow, or Fireworks

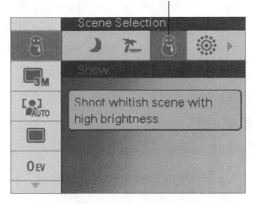

Figure 5-1: Scroll with the right arrow to find more scenes.

✓ **Panorama mode:** A *panorama* is an image that covers an especially wide area. For example, a normal photo of the Grand Canyon may not do justice to the tremendous expanse of its convolutions. The details of a large building may be lost if you squeeze them into a single shot. Panoramas are usually created by combining two or more photos — sometimes as many as half a dozen or more. If your camera doesn't have a Panorama mode, you can use photo-editing software to stitch photos together into a panorama. See the task, "Capturing a Panorama," later in this chapter.

✓ **Burst mode:** Because Burst mode captures many shots in rapid succession while you hold down the Shutter Release button, you may not need it when shooting (slow-moving) landscapes. Still, clouds move, the wind rearranges the scene before you, and even the light shifts from moment to moment. Burst mode may help you catch a special moment.

✔ **Flash mode**: Odds are that using a flash will be useless for most landscape shots because a flash has a limited range. However, if the flash is set to Auto, it may flash even when it does no good. Turn off the flash for landscapes, unless you're including a person or object close enough to benefit from additional light.

Taking a Landscape Photo

To take a landscape photo, follow these steps:

1. **Select Landscape mode on your camera.**

   Landscape mode is usually represented by a couple of triangular mountains.

2. **Press the Flash button repeatedly until the flash is off.**

3. **If your camera has zoom capability, start at the widest view (least amount of zoom) — press the W (Wide) end of the zoom switch, not the T (Telephoto) end.**

   Most cameras start at the widest view each time you turn on the camera. A few cameras, though, remember the zoom setting from the previous use.

   See the "Capturing a Panorama" section if you're shooting an especially expansive scene.

4. **Frame your photo.**

   If you can't make out details on the LCD, use the viewfinder, if you have one. Press the Finder/LCD switch to toggle the display between the LCD and the viewfinder. If you must use the LCD in bright light, look for landmarks within the frame to help compose your photo.

5. **If the subject is the sky, including clouds, place the horizon about one-third up from the bottom of the frame so that you have one-third Earth and two-thirds sky.**

   Alternatively, if the subject is the Earth, including mountains, place the horizon about one-third down from the top of the frame so that you have one-third sky and two-thirds Earth.

   This is part of photography's venerable Rule of Thirds. You can read more about this in Chapter 3.

6. **Take a photo or a few.**

7. **Consider moving to change your perspective. Try zooming in slightly — press the T (Telephoto) end of the zoom switch. Zoom in all the way for particularly distant shots.**

   Figure 5-2 shows a landscape taken with the widest setting and again zoomed in closer to the peak.

Widest setting

Zoomed in

Figure 5-2: Change your perspective.

Some landscapes work well in *portrait orientation,* where you rotate your camera left or right vertically 90 degrees. (Remember that portrait and landscape orientations are not the same as Portrait and Landscape modes.) A portrait orientation of a canyon or ridge that recedes from you may draw the eye into the picture more than the same scene in landscape orientation. Mix it up.

Shooting a Sunrise or Sunset

Be ready long before sunrise or sunset begins. Stay with the transition beyond twilight to full morning or night.

See aa.usno.navy.mil/data/ or www.sunrisesunset.com for rise and set times for the sun and the moon.

The following tips can help you when you're shooting a sunrise or sunset:

✔ Position the horizon about one-third of the way up the frame — one-third Earth, two-thirds sky.

✔ Don't shoot directly at the sun, especially when using the zoom — you'll just fry something in the camera. Place the orb off-center, one-third of the way from the left or right edge of the frame or off-frame altogether.

✔ If it's light enough to see details around you, use Landscape mode or Automatic. As details fade, try the Twilight or Low Light setting. If it's too dark to make out details, use Night Scene mode.

✔ If you're shooting a subject in front of the light, strong backlighting may cause the camera to *underexpose* the subject (making your photo too dark). If the subject is within range of your flash (about 12 feet), turn on the flash to force it to illuminate the subject. (Auto-flash mode may not trigger a flash if the camera is tricked by the bright background.)

✔ Look in the opposite direction of the sun. Sometimes, the best light at sunset or sunrise is on the objects behind you, such as trees, mountains, or buildings.

Taking Photos at Night

Night offers real challenges for photographers. How do you capture what little light there is from the moon or street lights? How do you avoid blurring a photo in the process, which is a common problem in photos taken in low light? These pointers can help:

✔ Use a tripod unless the area you're photographing is very well lit or in reach of your flash. The photo in Figure 5-3 was taken with a tripod. Even an iron grip might have blurred that photo, if taken hand-held.

Figure 5-3: This photo was taken using a tripod.

✔ Use the short timer (or a remote control) along with a tripod to eliminate any movement from depressing the Shutter Release button.

✔ Use Night Sky mode (often represented by a crescent moon icon) or other low-light modes.

✔ If you use a flash for a close subject at night, the background tends to be black. If the background has details you want to include in the shot, your flash may have an option called *slow-synchro,* which adjusts settings to give more time to capture the background.

Snapping City Scenes

Every town has its showcase architecture. Look for public squares and plazas, museums, libraries, courthouses, and schools, as well as parks. Don't be shy about looking like a tourist, even in your hometown. Figures 5-4 and 5-5 show two cities hemispheres apart (Quito and Louisville).

Photo credit: Merri Rudd

Figure 5-4: Every city has something interesting to photograph.

Photo credit: Merri Rudd

Figure 5-5: You can be creative in your hometown.

The following ideas will help you snap great photos of city scenes:

✔ Use Landscape mode or Automatic to focus on the entire scene.

✔ Get some distance to take in a large area of a cityscape: Shoot from a boat, a bridge, a skyscraper.

✔ Include crowds and traffic to convey the hustle and bustle of urban life.

✔ Shoot above crowds by setting the short timer. Press the Shutter Release button and hold the camera above your head at arms' length, while the timer takes the picture. (It helps to have an LCD that flips down in this case, so you can frame the photo.)

✔ Use a monopod in crowded settings where your camera needs extra stability but a tripod won't work.

✔ See the next section, "Capturing a Panorama," if you're shooting a particularly large building or other structure.

Capturing a Panorama

Many large subjects, such as landscapes or a building, look puny in a photo. Squeezing the full expanse of some scenes into one little frame seems to squeeze the essence out of the subject. In such cases, you may do better taking several pictures of portions of the scene. Later, in editing, you can stitch those photos together into one large photo that may better capture the majesty of the original. The key step is to overlap those multiple photos.

✔ Begin a panorama by planning where you will start and end taking pictures. You will take two to six photos in succession as you create the panorama. (A 360-degree panorama could involve a dozen or more photos.) Each photo must overlap the previous photo; that is, you'll include 20 to 30 percent of the same area in both photos.

✔ Use a tripod or keep the camera very steady and level throughout the shooting. Minimize vertical movement as you move the camera from left to right or right to left to take each shot for a horizontal panorama. If you're taking a vertical panorama (say, of a tall building), minimize horizontal movement as you move from the top down or the bottom up, overlapping each photo with the prior one.

✔ If your camera has a Panorama or Panorama Assist mode, select that mode from the scene dial or the menu.

Some cameras assist you in framing a panorama. You may see a grid. You may see arrows indicating the direction you should move after you take each photo. Some cameras show a portion of the previous photo as an overlay to help you align the next photo with the previous. If you're using Panorama mode, press the Menu or the OK button after you take the last photo to turn off Panorama mode.

✔ If your camera doesn't have a Panorama mode, take the individual photos as previously described. Be sure to overlap areas in each photo roughly 20 to 30 percent.

✔ As you take each photo, don't change any settings. Don't change the zoom, either.

✔ Some cameras automatically stitch the overlapping photos together to produce the panorama in the camera after you take a set number of photos or turn off Panorama Assist. With most cameras, you have to stitch the photos together yourself on a computer, using photo-editing software.

✔ Figure 5-6 shows a panorama stitched together from four photos. Many people crop the resulting panorama to eliminate the ragged areas above and below to make the panorama look more like a single photo, but I like the effect as you see it.

Figure 5-6: Stitch together photos to make a panorama.

Chapter 6

Ten Tips for Better Photos

*B*efore you begin shooting pictures, a few simple steps can ensure that your photos turn out as well as they can. After you've taken the shot, some simple edits can improve it even more. This chapter provides ten easy tips for getting better photographs.

Know Your Camera

To take pictures, all you really have to know is how to turn the camera on and confirm it is in fully Automatic mode. However, your camera is capable of much more, even if you don't use all of its features. Beyond the topics covered elsewhere in this book, here are a few more features to look for and adjustments you can make on your camera:

✔ Turn off digital zoom to avoid pixilation.

✔ Turn on image stabilization to avoid blurring.

✔ Turn off automatic flash to avoid unexpected flashes that may startle you or your subject. Automatic flash may go off pointlessly in landscapes or when using the zoom.

✔ Use exposure compensation to push a photo lighter or darker.

✔ Use white balance to compensate for fluorescent, incandescent, and other tinted light sources.

✔ Use the histogram display to analyze the distribution of light and dark (and to serve as a guide for exposure compensation).

Become One with Your Camera

The camera does you no good if you leave it somewhere else. Take your camera with you. Don't be afraid to look like a tourist or a camera geek. And the camera does you no good if it's turned off. Have the camera on, lens cap off, and be ready for the next great photo.

Even so, practice discretion. People may not want you to photograph them, so be considerate. Flowers and animals, on the other hand, seldom object. Point your camera down when you're not taking pictures.

Change Your Perspective

Move around as much as you can under the circumstances. Try crouching for shorter or lower subjects. Try holding the camera over your head to clear a crowd. (A tiltable LCD is very helpful in such cases.) Move left and right of the subject to try different angles. You'll discover interesting facets of the subject and new angles on the light. Photograph flowers up close with the light source behind them, but not directly, for interesting color and details.

Take Lots of Pictures

Aside from your initial investment for the camera, digital photos essentially cost you nothing. Go wild. Don't take a few photos, take dozens. Don't come back from vacation with 50 photos; come back with 500. Examine your photos for new ideas or mistakes in composition and exposure.

This liberation comes with an obligation: Don't expect anyone to look at every picture you take, no matter how much they love you. Before you show your photos to friends and family, select the better ones for show and skip (or delete) the less interesting ones. If you have five cool shots of a scene, pick the best, and maybe the second best, to show.

Back Up Your Photos

It should be a given with all digital data that you have a plan for frequent and regular backups. (Odds are you don't. No show of hands here.) There are many different schemes for backup — from full backups of the entire computer to selective backups of individual folders or files. The question is: What will you do when you change your mind about an edit or deletion? Move your files from the camera to the computer and back them up before you begin deleting or editing. Then back them up again after you've carefully organized, edited, and tagged them.

Learn to Edit

You can perform the most basic editing functions with tools you may already have or that you can download from the Web for free. These essential edits include rotating, cropping, and resizing photos. Much more sophisticated editing allows you to tweak individual pixels and completely transform a photo. Start with the basics and move on to fancier tasks when you're ready.

Share and Participate

If you like your photos, someone else will, too. Share your photos a few at a time by e-mail or in larger batches through a Web-based photo sharing site. Give back to your community by looking at other people's photos and commenting appropriately.

Add Metadata

Your camera automatically adds some additional information, called *metadata,* to each photo. This data includes date and time the photo was taken, camera settings used, and camera model information. Your photo organizer or editor enables you to add tags to describe the photo subject or location. Tag your photos as you copy them to the computer. Use those tags to quickly locate photos regardless of where they're stored or when you took them.

Use a Tripod

A tripod is a must for shooting under low light or with some longer lenses. A tripod is also quite handy for self portraits and group portraits. You may want a full-sized tripod, but everyone needs a pocket-sized version at a minimum.

Add Hardware Extras

Consumer cameras and most prosumer cameras don't take hardware add-ons other than tripods. All DSLRs can change lenses. You'll want a standard wide-angle lens and something for distance, either a fixed telephoto or a zoom lens. Look for lenses guaranteed to fit your particular camera's body.

Some lenses accept filters, which change some aspect of the light, such as tint or brightness. A polarizing filter can reduce reflections from water and glass and add depth to sky blue.

 Filters are made for specific lenses. Be certain to match the filter to your particular lens. Most consumer and prosumer models don't accept filters; all DSLR lenses do.

If you use an external, add-on flash, it may accept a diffuser to soften or distribute the light. You can also hold or position a separate reflector — a white or silver panel, oval, or even umbrella-shaped object — to reflect light onto a shaded area of the subject from any side.

Glossary

aperture: The resizable opening between the lens and the shutter that controls the amount of light entering the camera.

Aperture Priority mode: A camera mode that enables you to choose an aperture while the camera chooses the remaining settings.

Auto mode: A mode that enables the camera to make all necessary settings, such as focus, aperture, shutter speed, white balance, ISO, and flash.

bracket: To take several shots of the same subject using incremental adjustments to exposure settings for each shot.

Burst mode: Also referred to as continuous, or continuous drive, mode. Enables you to capture several images in rapid succession by pressing the shutter button only once.

composition: The positioning of the subject and surrounding area within the photo.

contrast: The difference in brightness between the light (highlight), dark (shadow), and middle (midtone) areas in an image.

crop: To eliminate excess area around a selected portion of an image.

depth of field (DOF): How much area is in focus in front and back of your subject. A shallow DOF results in a blurry background; and a deep DOF results in a sharp foreground, middle, and background.

DPI (dots per inch): A measure of the resolution of images; usually used in reference to printed images, printers, image setters, and other output devices.

DSLR (digital single-lens reflex): A style of camera body that accepts interchangeable lenses.

EVF (electronic viewfinder): The part of the camera you look through to shoot a photo. The EVF shows the scene plus camera settings.

exposure: The amount of light hitting the camera image sensor during image capture. Too much light results in an overexposed photo; too little light results in an underexposed photo.

filter: A framed glass or plastic disk placed over the lens to enhance the image capture in various ways. Also a tool in photo editing for changing all or part of a photo's exposure.

focal point: The position of the subject or the main point of interest in the scene.

grayscale: An image containing up to 256 levels of brightness from black to white.

image sensor: A light-sensitive computer chip that converts an image to a file.

ISO (Internal Organization for Standardization): A measurement of light sensitivity. A higher ISO setting increases light sensitivity; a lower ISO setting decreases the image sensor's sensitivity to light.

JPEG (Joint Photographic Experts Group): A file format and method of compression for digital photos. JPEGs use *lossy* compression that can result in image degradation when the image file is saved multiple times.

LCD (liquid crystal display): The LCD occupies much of the back of a camera and displays the scene plus camera settings, as well as menu options and previously taken pictures.

leading lines: Lines that draw the eye into a picture. Can be actual lines or lines implied by the composition of elements, such as a rolling hill or the horizon in a sunset shot.

lens: The part of the camera that focuses light before it passes through the aperture and shutter to strike the image sensor.

lossy/lossless compression: Indicates whether a data file, when compressed, will permanently lose data. In *lossy* compression, the file size is reduced by permanently eliminating some information. In *lossless* compression, all original data remains in the file when it is uncompressed.

Macro mode: A camera mode for shooting extreme close-ups.

Manual mode: A camera mode that lets you choose multiple camera settings simultaneously, such as shutter speed and aperture.

media card: *See* memory card.

megapixel: One million pixels.

memory card: Stores photos as they are taken. Memory cards come in types specific to different cameras and in various capacities measured in gigabytes or megabytes.

merger: A term for objects that appear to be physically extending out of people in a photo, such as telephone poles and trees.

metadata: Information about your digital file that is embedded in the image data. Includes such information as aperture, shutter speed, and date the photo was taken. Metadata can be viewed and edited in photo-editing software.

monopod: A pole or stick used to steady a camera.

noise: Unwanted graininess in an image, often caused by too little light, an overly high ISO setting, or other camera problems.

photo editor: A computer program that lets you fix or enhance digital photos.

photo organizer: A computer program that lets you organize, categorize, and label photos.

pixel: Abbreviation for *picture element*, the smallest component of a digital image.

RAW (or Camera RAW): A digital-photo file format that captures data from the camera's image sensor without internal processing.

red-eye: An undesirable red (or yellow or green) color, caused by a flash, that appears in the pupils of people and animals.

resolution: The measure of the number of pixels in an image. Usually expressed as width and height, such as 1024w x 768h.

Rule of Thirds: A compositional technique of dividing an image into vertical and horizontal thirds for an imaginary grid of nine equal segments and placing the focal point along one of the thirds or at one of the four grid intersections.

scene modes: The preprogrammed camera settings for specific scenes or contexts, such as Sports mode (for action) and Portrait mode (for close-ups).

Shutter Priority mode: A camera mode that enables you to choose a shutter speed while the camera chooses the remaining settings.

shutter speed: The length of time the shutter remains open, allowing light to hit the image sensor.

thumbnail: A small preview of an image, often used in digital imaging software.

TIFF (Tagged Image File Format): A file format for digital images often intended for printed output.

tripod: A three-legged stand used to hold and stabilize a camera, especially in low light.

USB (Universal Serial Bus): A connection port used to connect a device, such as a camera, to a computer.

viewfinder (VF): The part of the camera you look through to shoot a photo. The VF may be optical (glass or plastic) or electronic. *See* EVF.

white balance: A system of adjusting the exposure for lighting conditions such as incandescent or fluorescent light.

zoom lens: A lens that can adjust smoothly from wide angle (near) to telephoto (far). Super-zooms or ultra-zooms have the longest range.

After you've read the Portable Edition, look for the original Dummies book on the topic. The handy Contents at a Glance below highlights the information you'll get when you purchase a copy of *Digital Cameras & Photography For Dummies* — available wherever books are sold, or visit dummies.com.

Contents at a Glance

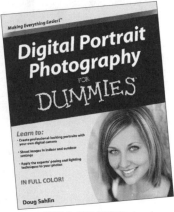